A People's Guide to Abolition and Disability Justice

Katie Tastrom

A People's Guide to Abolition and Disability Justice
© 2024 Katie Tastrom
This edition © 2024 PM Press

ISBN: 979–8–88744–040–8 (paperback)
ISBN: 979–8–88744–050–7 (ebook)
Library of Congress Control Number: 2023944272

Cover by John Yates / www.stealworks.com
Interior design by briandesign

10 9 8 7 6 5 4 3 2 1

PM Press
PO Box 23912
Oakland, CA 94623
www.pmpress.org

Printed in the USA.

Contents

Acknowledgments

This book was written primarily on Haudenosaunee Confederacy territory, and a portion of any money made will be donated to Haudenosaunee projects.

I want to thank Dr. Sydney Lewis for being my first reader and providing invaluable editorial assistance. (And also for being my favorite travel partner.)

I am also very grateful to my editors Charlie Allison and Wade Ostrowski and everyone else at PM Press who have made this process feel as smooth as possible (even when my writing was chaotic!).

Thank you to Springville Art Center for the space and time that are too hard to come by for those of us without fancy connections.

None of this would have been possible without the support of my partner, Shaun Tastrom Fenton.

There are so many people who have influenced the insights in this book, in big and small ways. I have learned so much through conversations, reading books and zines, and organizing with people around these topics for the last twenty-five years, and I am so grateful for their time and energy. However, I know if I try to name them here, I will spend the rest of my life being anxious about potentially leaving someone out! So this is a general thank-you to those folks who have done the work that I've learned from and who have taken me seriously enough to put time and effort into my political development.

Preface: COVID-19

A People's Guide to Abolition and Disability Justice is a book about COVID-19 that doesn't talk about it much. In the following pages, it's easy to see the scaffolding of institutions, policies, and structures that allowed a pandemic to be so deadly—especially to multiply marginalized disabled people—with those incarcerated at highest risk of serious complications and death.

I don't dive too deep into COVID here, because this book was written during the first couple of years of the ongoing pandemic, and things were changing quickly. Many of the specific policies I would have written about—such as criminalizing people for not wearing masks—would not have been as relevant by the time the book came out. The timing also meant that a lot of the resources and information I would need weren't available at the time. Even as this book is about to go to press, new information continues to come out about the consequences of decision-makers' mishandling of the pandemic. That said, COVID has been too devastating and relevant to the topics in this book to not give it its own section, albeit a brief one.

It Didn't Have to Be Like This
The US government's response to COVID-19 was both predictable and unconscionable. The pandemic laid bare the way health policy affects everything else, and the losses from COVID have not been felt equally by all communities. When adjusted for age, Indigenous, Latino, Pacific Islander, and Black American communities suffered significantly higher COVID mortality

rates than white and Asian ones.[1] It's not a coincidence either that the populations that are most at risk of incarceration are the same ones most likely to die of COVID: disabled people of color.[2] This is the outcome of decisions and policies that simultaneously abandon and surveil disabled people.

Prisons didn't appear out of thin air, and unfortunately they won't disappear that way either. Nothing about our current society was inevitable. We got here because of the choices that have been made, but this also means that different choices will lead to different outcomes. One of the recurring themes of this book is the importance of focusing on policy. To be clear, by "policy" I don't just mean laws passed by the government. I mean any kind of "rule" made by the people and organizations that have the power to enforce that rule. For example, whether a workplace allowed employees to work from home when the pandemic first hit is a policy choice. Policies, both formal and informal, have direct life-changing, life-limiting, and life-ending effects, including incarceration and death.

There are so many policies, big and small, that could have been implemented before and during COVID to make the pandemic less deadly. Some examples are: better health communication and education, prioritizing vulnerable people, providing income for people to be able to stay home, and not allowing pharmaceutical patents to be enforced.

Even before the pandemic, the lack of universal health insurance in the US caused unnecessary sickness, death, and incarceration, and COVID exacerbated this divide. One study found not only that people without health insurance were more likely to contract and die from the virus, but also that community insurance levels also affected COVID spread:

> Between the start of the pandemic and August 31, 2020—health insurance gaps were linked to an estimated 2.6 million COVID-19 cases and 58,000 COVID-19 deaths.... Each 10% increase in the proportion of a

county's residents who lacked health insurance was associated with a 70% increase in COVID-19 cases and a 48% increase in COVID-19 deaths.[3]

These statistics underscore what we knew even before COVID: the communities someone is a part of have a major impact on their health. Even individuals with health insurance who live in a neighborhood where residents are uninsured (i.e., poor and Black and Brown communities)[4] are at a greater risk of death. This is not because of some inherent difference, but because of policy decisions they had nothing to do with.

COVID-19 showed blatantly how those with the power to make decisions that affect others—like determining who has access to health care and who gets vaccines—are literally deciding which communities get to live and die. While the pandemic made it especially obvious, this isn't new. The whole carceral system in the US is one (huge) way those in power have decided who gets to live and participate meaningfully in their communities. Throughout the following pages, I examine some of the policies that have contributed to our current carceral state, especially the ways it targets disabled people.

COVID-19 and Incarceration

When you are in state custody, your literal life is at the mercy of decision-makers—people who you've probably never met and who (at best) simply don't care about your well-being. The pandemic proved this.

Writing for the Crunk Feminist Collective, Cara Page and Eesha Pandit explain:

> People being held in prisons, jails, and detention centers around the country are acutely at risk given that they are being held in spaces designed to maximize control over them, not to minimize transmission or to efficiently deliver health care.[5]

Disability and incarceration are strongly correlated, and throughout this book I discuss some of the ways the carceral system uses disability as a pretext to take control over the lives of not only disabled people but also nondisabled Indigenous, Black, Brown, queer, trans, and poor people, with multiply marginalized people always the most targeted. The reason the pandemic has been especially devastating for people who are locked up is because they are overwhelmingly disabled, which places them at a higher risk of dying or getting permanent illness from COVID if they contract it.

Logically, then, on a public health level if not an individual one, when COVID first hit, it would have made sense to prioritize the safety of those who are locked up in jails, nursing homes, and other places with large amounts of high-risk people living together. However, the opposite happened.

According to the COVID Prison Project, "The majority of the largest single-site outbreaks since the beginning of the pandemic have been in jails and prisons."[6] One of the many arguments for abolition is the way those in state "care" are sickened and killed. Infections are allowed to run rampant in these facilities because incarcerated people are seen as disposable, which I am calling "carceral epidemiology." (I promise this is the only term I make up throughout the entire book.)

Carceral Epidemiology

Carceral epidemiology is the way the state—by which I mean the government and other forms of formal and informal control, not one of the fifty states—uses communicable disease as part of the informal punishment of incarceration. While all congregate settings (places where a lot of people live together) have an increased risk of COVID-19 and other transmissible illnesses, in carceral locations the vulnerability to illness is a feature, not a bug. In other words, the risk of getting sick is an intentional aspect of the punishment. In part this is supposed to incentivize people to stay out of these places, as if anyone would be locked up if they had a choice.

Carceral epidemiology also devalues the lives of people who are incarcerated and institutionalized by failing to protect them from infection and seeing their illnesses and deaths as inevitable or even deserved. This was blatantly illustrated in the way vaccines were prioritized.

Even though people in jail and prison were at as much or higher risk than those in other congregate facilities, they weren't given access to the vaccine until much later. Though the specific prioritization order varied by state, one study found that "incarcerated people were consistently not prioritized in Phase 1, while other vulnerable groups who shared similar environmental risk received this early prioritization."[7]

The people who died and continue to die from COVID-19 aren't a random sampling of the population. They are disproportionately marginalized and institutionalized. When the government shirks its duty to keep people safe—both in times of emergency and in daily life—those who are already vulnerable pay the biggest price.

COVID Is Still Here

We didn't end up where we are in a vacuum. (This is true of both COVID and prisons.) COVID didn't need to be endemic, and decisions are still being made that will increase sickness and death for the most vulnerable. For example, in September 2022, President Joe Biden said COVID was "over," even though thousands of people in the US were still dying from it every week.[8] Melody Schreiber wrote about the deadly impact of Biden's comments for the *New Republic*:

> In order to avoid—or at least mitigate—what's likely to
> be another vicious winter wave, as many people need
> to get the updated boosters as possible. Now though,
> many people feel little urgency to do so—if they even

know the new shots exist. The funds to continue keeping Americans safe from Covid—including vaccines, treatments, and tests—are dwindling or extinguished.... Who needs to end a pandemic that's already done?[9]

Declarations like Biden's aren't just rhetorically frustrating, they have concrete negative effects. On April 10, 2023, Biden signed a congressional resolution that officially ended the COVID-19 "public health emergency," even though in the US over a thousand people were *still* dying of the virus every week.[10]

Formally ending the "public health emergency" means that many of the health measures implemented to keep people safe from COVID are ending. For example, Medicare (a public health insurance many disabled people have) has stopped covering free at-home tests, and PCR tests will also no longer be free.[11] While some health insurance plans will still cover testing, many uninsured people will have no access to free tests.

As long as the carceral state exists, it will always use health and disablement as weapons—from who gets access to vaccines, to the ways government neglect leads to "underlying conditions" that make COVID-19 more likely to be deadly, to being forced into congregate settings through laws that criminalize poverty, and on and on. These policies make the difference between life and death, freedom and captivity, and health and sickness. The pandemic underscores how important it is to understand the ways these systems affect disabled people, especially disabled people of color. The way the virus was handled in jails and prisons is yet more evidence of something that Indigenous and Black Americans know all too well: that even brief contact with the US criminal legal or carceral system can be a death sentence. This is just one of the many reasons why abolition is so necessary.

Throughout this book, I discuss more of the many policies that lead to disabled people being disproportionately incarcerated and killed. As you read, I encourage you to think about the ways government policies around COVID-19 have put disabled people at greater risk of illness and death, especially those incarcerated in prisons, jails, institutions, group homes, nursing homes, and other sites of detention.

Introduction

I hate this part of the book. It's where I'm supposed to explain to you why you should listen to me. Usually this is where the author lists their degrees and fellowships and appointments and where they have taught, or maybe their fancy friend writes six to eight pages about how brilliant the author is. I always find this funny in leftist books, especially the more we understand the importance of lived experience and the way the systems that give out grants and fellowships and tenure reward assimilation and punish radicalism.

I don't want you to listen to me because of my degrees or employment, because that's not where I've gained most of the knowledge I draw on for this book. Classrooms cannot compare to what I've learned from the times I've been sobbing in front of elevators that are "out of order," making whole buildings inaccessible, or the times of frustration in trying to find emergency mental health care for someone who needs more than a therapist appointment in three months but less than inpatient, as well as other times I've had to navigate systems—including the criminal justice system—for myself or someone else.

Though I have both an MSW (master of social work) and a JD (law degree), that's not the main source of my expertise. Most of my knowledge has come from other disabled people, especially disabled queer and trans and Black and Brown women and femmes. I've also learned a lot from my own experiences being on the targeted end of some of these systems (though my white and other privileges mean I escape the worst of it). I want to be clear that all of this knowledge is rooted in the genius of disability justice and those of us who are barely surviving, and emphatically not in the academy, which tends to do more harm than good. (But that's a different book.) Each chapter could easily be a whole book alone, and at some point I had to draw a line around what to include. Just know that I could say so much more about every single section, and don't assume there's not more context and exceptions than appear on the page.

This book aims to continue a radical lineage of abolitionist thought and draws on the work of many others, and thus I include a lot of citations and references. I also use many direct quotes, in part because I wanted to make sure that this direct heritage is obvious. Also, I wanted to draw a clear line between my analysis and the people I've learned from. Besides giving credit where credit is due, I want to give readers specific texts to go to so they can learn more.

Triggers
This book is (necessarily) full of potentially triggering content, and you should take care in reading. I tried to organize the book in a way that makes clear what kind of content appears in which section so readers can make their own decisions on how to navigate the book. I also focus largely on policy and avoid going into detail about well-known atrocities that there is a ton of information about (for example, the historical conditions of institutions for disabled people). While I felt that including some disturbing narratives was necessary to illuminate certain issues, I try to be mindful of the reader. Not because I think you can't handle it; it's actually the opposite. I am writing this book for people who may have been incarcerated or institutionalized themselves, or are close to people who have been, and know the subjects way too well.

Process
I wrote most of this book from bed. Usually my bed, but sometimes hotel beds when I was able to work, and sometimes an

Airbnb the rare times I could swing it. I relied on my prednisone, icing and heating my wrists, and a lot of weed to get these words onto these pages.

While my chronic illnesses and mental health disabilities provided material physical obstacles to completing this book, at the same time, none of it would have been possible if I weren't disabled. Most books of this scope and depth are written by college professors and other people who can access grants and other funding. By nature of their positions, these authors are often removed from interacting directly with these systems. This isn't universal, of course—and many exceptions are cited throughout—but in general, the more one bears the brunt of these systems, the harder it is to harness the multiple kinds of resources it takes to write a book like this.

As I noted in the preface, because of my fancy immune system I am especially high risk for COVID-19 complications, so most of this book was written while isolating in some manner from the virus. When the pandemic started, I was working as a sex worker, and having to isolate really limited my (already modest) income. Besides a stay at the Springville Arts Center—which I am extremely grateful for—there was no other organizational support for this project.

I say this because my (in)ability to access resources unsurprisingly affected the shaping of this book. For example, because I didn't have money, I did not interview as many people who have experienced these systems as I had initially planned. Instead, I relied almost totally on writing, which also had the benefit of being more accessible, as I didn't need to coordinate schedules with anyone, which is hard because of my fluctuating health.

Fortunately, I was able to get a ton of books and articles that I consulted for this project, though there were many that were too expensive for me to access. The books I did get were in large part thanks to friends (and some clients) buying them for me, which is something I would not have been able to do without the social capital I've acquired through the connections I've made in my decades involved in activism.

How to Use This Book

Use this book however it is most useful for you and your communities to work toward abolition and disability justice, whether that's as a bible or as toilet paper. Take what works for you and ignore the rest. I'm writing to my fellow disabled people, as well as disability justice activists, in beds and institutions and jails. That's who I hope will get the most out of this book. Of course, I want everyone to read it and incorporate it into their analysis, but I especially want people who are directly affected and terrorized by these systems to use the information here in any way that helps.

I hope to make it easier for people to move from abolitionist thought to action, and I want to give people the tools to do their own abolitionist analyses. I agree with abolitionist organizer and activist Mariame Kaba, who said:

> I don't think this is a work that is about experts. I want this work to be work that anyone and everyone who wants to try to do it does. And I don't want people to feel like this is work that you have to get some certification in, in order to be able to do.[1]

We can all work toward abolition and disability justice, and I hope both new and seasoned activists get something out of this book. The chapters end with a list of the foundational texts that laid the groundwork for each chapter. I also include a longer list of resources at the end of the book for further reading on the topics I discuss.

To be effective in uprooting them, we first need to understand who these systems target and how they work. Consider this book a humble—and inevitably flawed—offering toward that goal. I hope to do justice to all of the disabled people and abolitionists (often one and the same) who have built the ramps to get us where we are now. I would not be here writing a book in my bed in my own home without them. I probably wouldn't be here at all. I especially want to recognize Black-led liberation movements, like the movement for Black lives, which is responsible for making abolition something we can have a conversation this in-depth about. As I stress in the following chapters: both abolition and disability justice are incredibly racialized.

The overarching purpose of this book is to help abolitionists include disability justice concepts in their work, and I want mainstream disability organizations to understand the huge stake they have in abolition, and to begin working toward it.

Abolition Basics

We live in capitalism. Its power seems inescapable—but then, so did the divine right of kings. Any human power can be resisted and changed by human beings.
                                                    —Ursula K. Le Guin

Though the concept of prison abolition has been around as long as prisons have, there has been a recent increase in awareness, which is generally a good thing. The problem is that some of the people who talk about abolition don't necessarily know what they are talking about. Though often well intentioned, their misrepresentations (like the view that abolishing the police doesn't mean abolishing the police) have led to confusion and have allowed abolition to be watered down and co-opted by neoliberalism.

The political theories behind the prison and police abolition I write about in this book come from a radical Black feminist tradition created and inspired by abolitionist scholars and organizers like Angela Davis, Mariame Kaba, Ruth Wilson Gilmore, and many others. I'm only scratching the surface to provide a framework for my own analysis, and this is nowhere near complete or representative of the depth of wisdom that has already been shared on these topics. The goal of this chapter isn't to convince skeptics of abolition, but to provide the reader with a better understanding of abolition in general and some background for later chapters. So in addition to nuts and bolts, I discuss some of the history and concepts that further illuminate abolitionist thought.

What Is Abolition?

By abolition I mean the literal end of prisons, jails, police, and other carceral systems. "Carceral systems" are structures that have the power to imprison someone against their will, such as police, institutions, and hospitals—not just the physical structures, but also the policies, organizations, and other elements that make these systems function. As you make your way through this book, this will become much more concrete if it isn't already.

The following pages are full of reasons why we are calling for abolition, but in a nutshell, prisons aren't and never were about safety or accountability. Their function is to make money for a few elites and to maintain racial, class, and other hierarchies. In the 2003 book *Are Prisons Obsolete?* Angela Davis makes the case for the abolition of prisons by pointing out that prisons are a place where the elite hide the victims of their policies, explaining that they "relieve us of the responsibility of seriously engaging with the problems of our society, especially those produced by racism and, increasingly, global capitalism."[1]

Whether it's the ICE detention centers full of workers after NAFTA ended, prisons full of casualties of the "War on Drugs," or juvenile detention facilities full of kids who were poisoned by the lead in their neighborhoods, prisons (and I would argue institutions, group homes, and other places where people are locked up against their will) are where we dispose of the victims of capitalism.

Yes, Even the "Violent" People

Just like history is written by the victor, violence is defined by the jailer. Our ideas of what constitutes "violence" and what doesn't are deeply influenced by capitalism and white supremacy.

Even an article posted on the US Department of Justice's own website admits:

> The criminal justice system fails to protect people from the most serious dangers by failing to define the dangerous acts of those who are affluent as serious crimes and by failing to enforce the law vigorously against affluent persons.[2]

Certain kinds of violence are punished, but other kinds are not. As I write this, Donald Trump has been indicted for various crimes, but none of the indictments address the way Trump's COVID policy led to so many unnecessary deaths. My point isn't that more things should be criminalized, but that the decision to criminalize some things and not others is not always based on the amount of harm they cause.

That's why it's important for those of us who want to reduce violence (especially against the most marginalized) to distinguish between crimes and harms. "Crime" is contextual, as marijuana laws show. Currently, in some states in the US, possession of even small amounts of marijuana is a crime that can lead to incarceration. In others, the state sells it directly. (In both scenarios, the state makes money.) Just because something is a crime doesn't necessarily mean that it's causing harm, and vice versa.

"Crime" isn't synonymous with moral failings or character flaws or even causing damage. If you are driving across the country with weed in your car, you don't suddenly become a different person when you are driving through the states where it is criminalized. Your conduct is the same, but in one place you are a committing a crime and in another you're not.

Of course, there are many things that are both crimes and harms, and harm is usually the rationale for criminalization. But there are also lots of harms that aren't crimes, especially harms perpetuated by the state. The most devastating harms— like war and climate change—are caused by people who are never charged with crimes. George W. Bush is retired and painting, while over one million people are dead from the Iraq invasion alone.[3]

There are also less extreme examples, many of which are detailed in the following chapters, because this book is largely about the state-perpetuated and -sanctioned violence that targets disabled people. Criminal laws do not exist in a vacuum; they were not handed down by a deity. It's not a coincidence that the people who make the criminal laws are the least likely to have their harms punished by the system.

Laws are not mountains that have been here before we were and will be here long after. They are more like water, changing over time and circumstances. Laws were created by people no different from most, except that they have the privilege and power to make the laws.

Safety

Many people's first reaction to the idea of abolition is fear. They worry about their safety and that of their family, because US culture teaches us that police and prisons help keep us safer. (Other cultures teach this too, but the US is where my expertise is, so that is where I am focusing, though I hope the principles can be useful for everyone.) While this reaction is understandable, it's not rational. It's factually and concretely untrue that police and prisons make us safer, and it's especially not true for disabled people.

Police Don't Make Us Safer

As I discuss below, the purpose of police and prisons was never safety. At best it's the safety of a few at the expense of others, but the purpose of policing was (and arguably still is) the caging of mostly racialized disabled bodies for the financial gain of rich white people. One question that people have about abolition is how we will be safe without police. This assumes that police stop or prevent crime, which isn't true. Police don't make us safer.

At their very best, police are useless. In *The End of Policing*, Alex S. Vitale wrote about how little police usually do:

Felony arrests of any kind are a rarity for uniformed officers, with most making no more than one a year. When a patrol officer actually apprehends a violent criminal in the act, it is a major moment in their career.[4]

Many people believe that if they face violence, they can call the police, who will then arrive and stop the violence, but that's not true at all. As Vitale points out, most officers barely make felony arrests to begin with, and most will never stop someone in the act of committing violence in their whole career. So if police aren't out apprehending felons, how do they spend their time? The majority work in patrol, which for the most part means walking or driving around and arresting and ticketing for petty things like drug possession or traffic violations. There are also other duties, like taking reports, directing traffic, and so on, but none of these justify the existence of the police, and they would be done better and more cheaply by almost any other structure.

Cops do not make communities safer, because they were never intended to. Scholars have found that there is no correlation between the number of police and crime rates.[5] In an essay titled "Concentrating Punishment: Long-Term Consequences for Disadvantaged Places," Daniel Cooper and Ryan Lugalia-Hollon explain the myth that some communities are arrested more because they commit more crimes:

> In theory, high incarceration rates in [certain areas] can simply be explained by levels of crime. But no such simple correlation exists. Crime is not a pure predictor for levels of imprisonment.... Communities that experienced high disadvantage experienced incarceration more than three times higher than communities with a similar crime rate.[6]

This is an extremely important point. The more I learn about all this, the more it has become clear that your chances of being arrested have little to do with what you do and much more to do with who you are and the circumstances you were born into. People with a lot of privilege can do anything and not get arrested, while multiply marginalized folks can do everything perfectly and end up involved in the system.

Emergencies

So what would happen in an emergency if the police didn't exist? Well, first let's compare that to what happens now in the vast majority of cases, which is that they get there too late to be helpful and then do nothing.

As discussed above, police don't stop crime. It's rare for one of them to interrupt a crime in progress and help make people safer. It makes so much more sense to work with the people around you to keep each other safe, if for no other reason than that in an emergency those are the people who can help most quickly.

In an interview in *Bitch* magazine, Mariame Kaba suggests creating relationships with the people around us so that we can respond when there is an issue without having to call the police. Kaba says:

> Let's work on building that, whether it's building new skills or developing a new social relationship with our neighbors—the proactive things that we ought to be doing all the time so we can be responders to the harms that occur in our communities. Maybe you have a phone tree in your building so if you heard something like [interpersonal violence in a neighboring apartment], you know who to call and ask, "Are you hearing this too? Maybe we should go together." There are concrete ways of trying to intervene.[7]

There is not one solution to violence, there are many—and this is just an example. The whole point of abolition is that it's not one size fits all, because different situations call for different strategies. Talking and organizing with your neighbors may seem scary at first, because we are taught that the people outside our nuclear family are dangerous and police make things safer. However, it's just not true. Our immediate instincts about danger aren't always accurate, and they are highly influenced by the culture.

Prisons Also Don't Make Us Safer

Like with policing, prisons don't make us safer.[8] Studies show that long-term prison sentences are counterproductive for public safety.[9] There is more incarceration in low-crime areas with low education levels and little capital investment than there is in high-crime areas that have fewer indications of being disadvantaged.[10] Neighborhoods that have high incarceration levels don't necessarily have more crime, just more surveillance. Imprisonment doesn't reduce crime, it increases it, especially when you include the crimes committed by the state itself.

Part of the reason incarceration is so devastating is that it weakens not just family relationships but also community safety. Cooper and Lugalia-Hollon note that incarceration weakens the neighborhood bonds that—unlike police and prisons—have been found to actually reduce crime.[11] So not only do prisons and police have their own negative effects on public safety, but they also make it more difficult for neighborhoods to implement ideas that will actually lead to safety.

Disabled People Are Safer without Prisons, Police, and Other Carceral Systems

Though we are all safer without police and prisons, disabled people especially benefit. As I talk about at length in this book, the biggest threats to our health and safety aren't random strangers who are going to murder us. (Although it happens, it's very rare.) Instead, we are overwhelmingly harmed by systems and institutions and family members and caregivers—the kinds of perpetrators who rarely end up in jail or prison.

Disabled people are being harmed in myriad ways by these systems, and even if we didn't have anything better (we do! keep reading!) it would still be safer for there to be no prisons or police. About half of the people killed by police were identified as being disabled.[12] (I put it that way because as I detail in the next chapter, "disability" can mean many things. I think the researchers' definition may be more limited than how we usually think of disability, and the percentage is probably even higher.)

Many of the most publicized victims of police violence were disabled. Charleena Lyles was known to have mental health disabilities when the police killed her in front of her four young children in Seattle in 2017.[13] A few years earlier, in New York in 2014, Eric Garner—who had asthma, diabetes, and a heart condition—was murdered by a police officer.[14] Freddie Gray had been diagnosed with developmental disabilities caused by environmental racism before being killed in Baltimore in 2015.[15] (It's important to note that all of these people were both Black and disabled, an intersection that will come up constantly when we talk about who is targeted by these systems.)

I could go on and on, but I'm sure you already know of many others. The majority of the victims of police violence we hear about are disabled.

It's also common knowledge that people in jail and prison disproportionately have mental health issues. The Prison Policy Initiative found:

> People with multiple arrests were 3 times more likely to have a serious mental illness (25% vs. 9%) and 3 times more likely to report serious psychological distress, including symptoms of depression and anxiety, than people with no arrests in the past year (30% vs. 11%).[16]

The actual number is probably much higher, and it's not debatable that disabled people are disproportionately victimized by incarceration and police violence, especially multiply marginalized disabled people. As such, anyone focused on police violence must also consider disability, and disabled people have a vested interest in police abolition. We all know that something is going on with disability and prisons, but we don't often look closer at what this means for both disabled people as individuals and carceral systems as a whole.

As I show throughout this book, the people in prison are overwhelmingly just disabled people who are locked up because of some (and often all) of the intersections of disability, poverty, race, and capitalism. Whether or not someone will be incarcerated isn't a matter of behavior but rather of who is being targeted and surveilled.

When Disabled People Are Incarcerated

Prisons and jails are bad. Especially so for disabled people. One reason is because they spend more time locked up than nondisabled people arrested for the same offenses.[17] Disabled people behind bars are also more likely to face disciplinary action and consequences. Liat Ben-Moshe explains:

> For those who are incarcerated and are directly unable or seen as unable to "follow orders," which is a critical aspect of surviving in a carceral locale, including those with hearing, intellectual, or psych disabilities, the ability to move between tiers and regain more privileges is much diminished. One of the implications is that those incarcerated spend much of their sentences in various levels of solitary confinement, which is likely to lead to mental and physical disablement.[18]

Solitary confinement is literally torture, because of the destructive effect it has on people's mental health.[19] For people who already have disabilities, the isolation will cause quick decompensation:

> The stress, lack of meaningful social contact, and unstructured days can exacerbate symptoms of illness

or provoke recurrence. Suicides occur disproportionately more often in segregation units than elsewhere in
prison. All too frequently, mentally ill prisoners decom-
pensate in isolation, requiring crisis care or psychiatric
hospitalization. Many simply will not get better as long
as they are isolated.[20]

Deteriorating the mental health of already disabled
people makes them less able to follow the rules. This is important, because solitary confinement is justified as a way to get
incarcerated people to comply, but it does the opposite.

The conditions in jails and prisons are uniformly horrible,
and they are especially harsh on disabled people. However, I
don't focus a lot on them here, because then the next step in
the conversation becomes about making jails and prisons more
accessible, which is not the goal. Prisons and jails are inherently harmful to disabled people. Trying to "improve" prisons
just puts more money into the criminal justice system, which
legitimizes it and allows it to continue to grow, making imprisoning disabled people even easier.

That doesn't mean that we don't want to work in solidarity with disabled people on the inside to get them what they
need to live as humanely as possible, including better medical
care and other things that make their lives easier. For example, I've assisted on cases where someone needed permission
from the prison to use their electric wheelchair instead of a
manual one. The manual one required relying on others to
go to the restroom, and when someone wasn't available the
person would be forced to soil themselves. Getting permission
to be able to use their electric wheelchair makes things better
for them without making the system bigger or pretending like
there is such a thing as "humane" prisons.

As I explain in much more depth in the chapters to come,
disability justice requires leadership of the most affected,
which means working in solidarity with those on the inside.

Abolitionists sometimes get into theoretical debates about how much energy we should put (if any) into the current conditions of imprisoned people. But in my experience, the two are rarely in conflict in practice, and there are usually ways to support people currently imprisoned without strengthening the system. Everyone is on the same side—the freedom one—and it's important to support the families most impacted by incarceration. An abolitionist analysis requires being thoughtful about the ways the entire system is implicated, and a big part of this is teasing out what we need to do to bring about the world we want.

Why Eliminating Mass Incarceration Isn't Enough

"Mass incarceration" isn't the problem, incarceration itself is. Dylan Rodríguez explains the problem with focusing on it:

> The post-racial euphemism of "mass incarceration" miserably fails to communicate how the racist and anti-Black form of the U.S. state is also its paradigmatic form, particularly in matters related to criminal justice policy and punishment. Put another way, there is no "mass incarceration." The persistent use of this term is more than a semantic error; it is a political and conceptual sleight of hand with grave consequences; if language guides thought, action, and social vision, then there is an urgent need to dispose of this useless and potentially dangerous phrase and speak truth through a more descriptive, thoughtful, activist history.[21]

"Mass incarceration" makes it sound like a problem that affects everyone, but some populations (rich and white and abled) are barely touched by these systems. Meanwhile, Black, Indigenous, and other communities of color lose family members to carceral systems—and the effects of these systems—constantly.

As Rodríguez points out, it's not a random subset of the

population who is being incarcerated, and that needs to be highlighted. It is disproportionately multiply marginalized people, usually disabled in some way (and as I explain later, if you are not disabled when you get locked up, you will be soon, because these places are intentionally disabling). Disabled people of color are especially targeted in the US, and this should be in the forefront of our minds when we talk about the increasing scope of the criminal justice system.

Colonization, Blackness, and the Growth of the Carceral State

Part of the reason prisons and policing are so ineffective for public safety is because they were never created to make anyone safer—they were created to make people money. You can draw a straight line from the current prison system back to the colonization of what is now called North America by white Europeans starting in the late 1400s and continuing today. Colonization is the process of foreign powers establishing control over Indigenous land and people. When they arrived in what is now called North America, European colonists engaged in a ceaseless campaign of genocide, torture, and removal, which led to the deaths and displacement of countless Indigenous people.

The legacy of colonization continues, as Indigenous people are incarcerated in the US at more than double the rate of white people.[22] One of the people interviewed for the American Indian Policy Center's *Searching for Justice: American Indian Perspectives on Disparities in Minnesota Criminal Justice System* study explains:

> Why do Indians go to jail? And that's basically from, that stems from almost three hundred years ago, from the culture. Think, what happened to our forefathers was a really bad thing, and through the generations have been traumas and traumas and traumas that have been carried over and carried over. And then multiplied by

the shockwaves that came after that, which hit us bad
in the boarding school days.[23]

Even a quick look at the history of Indigenous people in
what is now called North America shows continuous atrocities
by people of European descent. This includes the "boarding
schools" that the speaker referenced, where Indigenous children were stolen from their families and brought to residential
camps where they were tortured and killed.[24] The stated aim of
these schools was to "kill the Indian and save the man." These
concentration camps aimed to completely erase Indigenous
people and culture. The white adults who worked there would
beat children for speaking their language, and many children
died from their injuries, preventable and treatable illnesses,
and starvation. Generations were killed and traumatized, and
now their descendants are locked up in prisons and institutions
(and traumatized and killed).

Beyond the important ways that disability and criminalization affect individual Indigenous people, there's also a
more theoretical aspect to colonization. What is assumed to be
universal is often actually culturally specific to white western
and northern Europeans, which due to colonization has been
exported around the world. These values tend to be based in
capitalism, such as a focus on competition instead of cooperation or even the idea of "owning" land in the first place. The
colonization of the Americas and the genocide of Indigenous
people has effects that ripple through to today in ways that are
generally unacknowledged, including what we see as possible
for society.

You can see how we are fish in colonization's water in the
way that some people talk about "human nature," as if we exist
in a vacuum instead of in a society with a specific history that
cannot be separated out from some kind of "pure" humanity.
Our current situation was not inevitable, and the future will
be determined by the choices that are made now.

We need to ground our disability and abolition in decolonization, which includes learning from Indigenous sources and identifying the ways that colonization has affected our beliefs about what's possible. Indigenous communities have a long, continuing history of resistance that we can work in solidarity with.

Policing and Chattel Slavery

Policing is directly tied to chattel slavery. The purpose of policing originally was (and still is) to protect the property of rich people, which included enslaved humans. In *Becoming Abolitionists*, Derecka Purnell explains how policing began as a way for slaveholders to prevent rebellions:

> In the late 1600s, officials there legally mandated that every white man between sixteen and sixty join the militia, and legally empowered every white person to arrest, punish, and return runaways. White civilians were not only encouraged to monitor and control Black people, but were *required* to do so—sometimes under the threat of being fined. The government criminalized people for *not* policing.[25]

Modern-day policing comes directly from this overtly racialized system based on slave catching. "Abolition" is an intentional choice of language to connect modern-day policing and prisons to the chattel slavery they were created to uphold.

Prisons as Legal Slavery

I opened this chapter with the Le Guin quote to remind us that just as there was a time before prisons, there can be a time after. Anything that has been created can be destroyed, and anything that is needed can be built.

Prisons didn't become the primary mode of punishment in the US until the nineteenth century. Not coincidentally, they grew in popularity after the Thirteenth Amendment was ratified in 1865, outlawing slavery except as punishment for a crime. This huge loophole allowed enslavers and other rich white people to continue to extract unpaid labor from supposedly "free" African-descended people through the convict lease system.

Even though slavery was technically over, the convict lease system allowed county jails and state prisons to "rent out" imprisoned people to private businesses for labor, which incentivized locking up as many people as possible. V. Camille Westmont wrote about how convict leasing was designed specifically as a workaround for the prohibition of slavery:

> The convict lease system was not just an economic lifeline for cash-strapped Southern states at the end of the war; it was a political tool that enabled wealthy and elite white Southerners to maintain the racial and economic systems Emancipation was intended to dismantle.[26]

Newly "free" slaves would be convicted of (often fictional or minor) crimes and then sentenced to work without compensation, sometimes at the same plantations where they had been enslaved.

This exception to the prohibition of slavery becomes especially broad when you realize that often the same people who owned slaves were the ones who made the laws determining what was or was not a crime. Writing for Literary Hub, Jefferson Cowie described how little things changed and how closely aligned the increase in Black imprisonment was to the supposed abolishment of slavery:

> Back when African American "crime" had been the responsibility of masters and plantation managers, Black people represented zero percent of the prison population. As Reconstruction collapsed, however, the Black conviction rate rapidly rose. African Americans made up 8 percent of the total convict population in

1871, leaping to 88 percent in 1874, and then 91 percent in 1877. And the mines boomed.[27]

The Thirteenth Amendment's loophole was big enough to build the world's largest prison system in. We are where we are today because of where we came from. One of the reasons reforms don't work is because there is no (or little) change in the actual power of marginalized people. This allows the government to continue playing rigged three-card monte with the freedom of Black people, and incarceration is their deck.

It's not a coincidence that it is the descendants of enslaved and colonized people who are most disproportionately imprisoned. That's why in *The Nation on No Map: Black Anarchism and Abolition*, William C. Anderson argues that emancipation of slavery is a myth for a lot of Black people:

> Emancipation was a nonevent because enslavement continued despite an announcement it was ending. It was transformed into sharecropping and convict leasing and eventually found new life in the prison system.[28]

While white people are obviously imprisoned too, incarceration has always been a tool of white supremacy. The growth and reliance on prisons was a way to placate white liberals and still get the economic benefits of slavery. The seeds of the current carceral state were planted centuries ago, and their growth runs deep. Like invasive weeds, the only way to keep them from killing everything is to rip them up by the roots.

Sexual Violence

I'm conflicted about separating out sexual violence from the other sections, because I don't want to give the appearance that sexual violence happens in a bubble away from other violence. It doesn't. But I ultimately decided to have a separate section to make it easy to skip if it's too triggering or intense. Other chapters are just as potentially triggering, of course, which is why I separated them in a way that attempts to make clear the main topics in each one.

Sexual Violence by Police

Police are much more likely to perpetrate sexual violence than they are to do anything to protect someone from it.[29] The law gives police a ton of discretion and a lot of leeway for misconduct, and they often go past that. In some places, police are allowed to have sex with suspected sex workers as part of prostitution stings.

An article in the *California Law Review* states:

> The immediate problem PSV [Police Sexual Violence] presents is that it is not made clearly illegal by state law and police department regulation. The deeper problem is that PSV is a symptom of broader cultural problems within police departments.[30]

Andrea J. Ritchie's *Invisible No More: Police Violence against Black Women and Women of Color* discusses the myriad ways that police are violent against women of color, including sexual violence.[31] Even beyond the rampant racist and sexist abuse by individual officers, Ritchie points out that the entire structure of policing is conducive to unchecked violence against the most marginalized. For example, since police do most of their work alone or in pairs without a lot of direct oversight, they are able to perpetuate sexual violence much more easily than most other professions.

Law enforcement preys on victims without social and political power, such as sex workers, disabled people, people of color, queer and trans people, and homeless people, because they know that the power differential makes it almost certain they won't have any consequences from this behavior, including simply being stopped.

As a sex worker, I'm much more scared of the police than I am of clients, and studies back me up.[32] In our calculation of safety, we need to always take into account the violence the police do, not only as individuals, but also in the harms that are systemically facilitated by policing. There are no "good" apples when the tree is poisonous. Violence against women, including sexual violence, wasn't something that US culture took seriously, until the women's movement of the 1960s and 1970s brought domestic and sexual violence into mainstream conversation. However, because the activists were overwhelmingly white and middle class, their unrecognized privileges led to a version of "feminism" that is especially harmful to multiply marginalized women.

Carceral Feminism

Carceral feminism is a neoliberal approach to "safety" that throws everyone besides white abled cis women and men under the bus for the "safety" of a few privileged people. In an essay called "Against Carceral Feminism," Victoria Law explains and critiques carceral feminism:

> This carceral variant of feminism continues to be the predominant form. While its adherents would likely reject the descriptor, "carceral feminism" describes an approach that sees increased policing, prosecution, and imprisonment as the primary solution to violence against women.
>
> This stance does not acknowledge that police are often purveyors of violence and that prisons are always sites of violence. Carceral feminism ignores the ways in which race, class, gender identity, and immigration status leave certain women more vulnerable to violence and that greater criminalization often places these same women at risk of state violence.[33]

One example of carceral feminism that Law points out is the Violence against Women Act (VAWA). VAWA is a 1994 law (which was reauthorized in 2022) sold under the guise of protecting women from violence. Instead, its main effect is to provide more resources to law enforcement, including funding for one hundred thousand more police officers.[34] This increases state violence against the women the law is supposedly designed to help.

Other VAWA policies, like mandatory arrest laws, don't just increase state violence, they also increase interpersonal violence. These laws require the police to make an arrest whenever they are called to intervene in family violence situations. This takes the power out of survivors'—and even the police's—hands. The end result is that survivors end up in a lot more danger because they are afraid to call anyone and be forced into consequences they don't want.[35]

The truth is, we know how to decrease this kind of violence: give people resources. Law writes:

> At the same time, politicians and many others who pushed for VAWA ignored the economic limitations that prevented scores of women from leaving violent relationships. Two years later, Clinton signed "welfare reform" legislation. The Personal Responsibility and Work Opportunity and Reconciliation Act set a five-year limit on welfare, required recipients to work after two years, regardless of other circumstances, and instated a lifetime ban on welfare for those convicted of drug felonies or who had violated probation or parole.[36]

Carceral feminism ignores the role that state violence plays in the lives of everyone who isn't a wealthy white cis abled binary woman. Whenever we talk about safety, we need to ask ourselves whose safety we are prioritizing.

Among its many problems, carceral feminism also just doesn't work from a public safety perspective. As I explained above, more police and prisons don't make us safer.

The biggest threat to the safety of the white women the lawmakers pretend to care about "protecting" is not the people of color and disabled people who are being incarcerated, but the white men who are in their homes with them. This isn't unique to white cis women, as violence usually takes place between people who have an existing relationship, and we tend to have relationships with people who are similar to us (in large part because of the continued segregation exacerbated by carceral systems).

In "Do We Want Justice, or Do We Want Punishment? A Conversation about Carceral Feminism between Rachel Caïdor, Shira Hassan, Deana Lewis, and Beth E. Richie," Caïdor says:

> White supremacy and carceral feminism feed each other—only when you occupy whiteness in a certain way or you aspire to whiteness in a certain way do you have the luxury of deluding yourself that the laws of this country will work *for* you, not against you. To walk around and feel like the state is somehow out to protect you is the white supremacist weird programming that we've all been raised with. That programming comes from white supremacy, because the white supremacy really needs us to believe that the state and the way that its laws work are going to protect all of the people. But that's actually just not true.[37]

Carceral feminism harms the most marginalized women and girls (not to mention other gender minorities). Instead of saving people from violence, carceral feminism increases violence both by state and nonstate actors.

How Carceral Feminism Especially Fucks Over Disabled People

Disabled people are both disproportionately victims of sexual violence and disproportionately negatively affected by carceral feminist responses to sexual violence. Sexual violence doesn't exist separately from other forms of violence, and sexual violence is rampant in prisons and jails.[38] I still sometimes hear people make jokes (jokes!) about incarcerated people being raped. Since disabled people are targeted disproportionately by the criminal justice system, carceral feminism's reliance on policing and prisons makes disabled people more vulnerable to sexual violence through incarcerating them and simultaneously discouraging other approaches to prevent sexual violence.

Even outside of incarceration, disabled people are more likely to have experienced sexual violence than nondisabled people. This is true for children as well. GenerationFIVE, a group that calls for a "liberatory approach to child sexual abuse and other forms of intimate and community violence," explains:

> Child sexual abuse is also woven in with the systemic targeting of people who live with physical, cognitive, psychological, and learning disabilities. Broadly, people with disabilities are sexually assaulted at nearly three times the rate of people without disabilities, and disabled children and adults are twice as likely to be victims of child sexual abuse.[39]

We are conditioned to believe that law enforcement is the only way to respond to harm. This is not so: there are a lot of ways to respond to harm that don't rely on carceral systems.

Restorative and transformative justice, for example, are ways to address harm with affected individuals after the harm occurs.

Restorative justice is an approach that focuses on healing the damage that was done without the involvement of the state. Restorative justice is about repairing the harms done to an individual or community. Transformative justice is similar to restorative justice in that it intentionally avoids engagement with the state. What distinguishes transformative from restorative justice is that transformative justice also acknowledges the role that society plays. Transformative justice includes an aspect of changing the societal conditions that contributed to the harm as well.

While there is an important conceptual difference between the two terms, in my experience, the terms *restorative justice* and *transformative justice* are often used interchangeably in practice. Both approaches acknowledge that the state doesn't promote accountability or safety.

(While restorative and transformative justice are important parts of abolition to understand, I am skipping over them beyond this mention because I am focusing on systems and policies in this book, but I recommend learning more about these crucial abolitionist concepts to address interpersonal harm.)

Abolitionist Principles

All of this chapter is an overview, and I encourage further reading about abolition by checking out the Foundational Sources section at the end of each chapter and the Resources section at the end of the book, or seeking out other material about it. It's hard to summarize something based on such a large body of knowledge. (Just look how many "Resources" there are, and that is not even all of them!) I want to be completely clear that this chapter is nowhere near comprehensive, and these concepts aren't even necessarily the most "important" ones in abolition, but they are the ones I think are useful to lay the groundwork for the concepts I will discuss later.

"Abolition is not about your fucking feelings." —Mariame Kaba[40]

Abolition is not a personal development project. It's not a self-help course that will lead you to spiritual enlightenment. Abolition is about materially freeing people. You don't need a pure heart or to never feel any ill will toward people. I'm a bitch. I love reality TV because I like watching rich people be unhappy. All abolition requires is understanding that those instincts shouldn't be the basis for social policy. Some abolitionists say that we need to abolish the cops in our heart, and I don't necessarily disagree, but this book is focused on the cop on the street.

Carceral systems are called that because they are directly related to forms of incarceration. As I explain in later chapters, the lack of adequate benefits leads to disabled people being arrested, and therefore the current benefit system is carceral. Social relationships are not carceral unless someone has the power of the state in some way. There may be exceptions, but I believe abolition requires focusing on how the state wields power much more than on how we wield power socially. If we take the state out of the analysis, we're not talking about abolition.

I also don't care what you consume. Our power as consumers is much smaller than our collective political power. In other words, even if everyone consumed as perfectly as possible under capitalism, buying and not buying all the "right" things, these systems would still keep chugging along. We need to think about how our work actually impacts these systems, whether through tearing down or building things that are incompatible with carceral systems.

Prevention

Abolition doesn't just affect what we do *instead* of carceral systems, it affects our need for them in the first place. Instead of being reactionary, abolition focuses on being proactive and tries to prevent harm from occurring in the first place. The criminal justice system theoretically only applies after someone has already been harmed, though it makes more sense (and usually takes fewer resources) to prevent harm than to let it happen and then punish the wrongdoer. I have so many examples in this book of disabled people being harmed, and they were all preventable. We put so many resources into punishment and so few into prevention. There will always be conflict and harm, but as a society we should work to mini-mize it instead of focusing on merely getting vengeance after the fact.

Both/And

One of the barriers that a lot of people have with understand-ing abolition is that there is not a one-sentence answer to what will replace prisons, nor should there be. Abolition is a whole change of worldview. It moves us from "How do we replace prisons?" to "How do we create a world without carceral systems?" This requires not just tearing down structures, but also building resources that are more just and better suited to solve our problems.

One thing I learned in social work school was that it's harder for people to work toward a negative goal ("Stop doing x") than it is for them to work toward a positive goal ("Start doing y"). So, the best way to eliminate something is to increase other things that are incompatible or mutually exclu-sive. For example, if we want people out of coercive mental health treatment, one thing that helps is creating liberatory mental health resources.

The issue of abolition isn't actually "How do we get there?" but really "Where do we start?" Lots of us are already doing work that is incompatible with the carceral state, but we need to make sure it's grounded in abolition. In other words, we can all incorporate abolition into our corners of the world. It's not one or the other, it's both/and.

The world we are in is different than the world we are creating. We will falter and make mistakes, as well as do things that aren't mistakes but are the best alternatives out of bad options. While we need to be strict in our systemic analysis (i.e., look closely and critically at every aspect of the carceral system we live in), we need to be flexible and compassionate when we are dealing with each other as we work toward abolition by targeting systems.

Abolition both acknowledges the way carceral systems have hurt all of us (though some more than others, of course) and also understands that the way out of it is through systemic and political change, not just individual relationships.

Risk

Abolition is a risk, and risks involve danger. However, this danger is less than the danger that currently exists. The analogy I like to use is flying compared to driving. Lots of people have a fear of flying, while way fewer have a fear of driving, even though flying is statistically much less dangerous. Yet because we are used to cars, they feel less scary, and so we don't weigh those risks as heavily. My point being: our feelings aren't necessarily rational, and we tend to discount the risks of the status quo and inflate the risks of the unfamiliar.

While of course people should be able to drive if they choose (and anxiety is real!), we shouldn't make policy from what our *instincts* are but instead from what the *facts* are. And abolitionists have the facts on our side. In terms of individual risk, people tend to overstate the harm of neighbors and community and understate the harm of police. Your neighbor is less of a risk to you than the cop you call on your neighbor, in almost all circumstances.

There *is* risk involved in knocking on your neighbor's door to ask them to turn down the music, but it's *less* risk than calling the police. (I'm leaving aside options like ignoring it to make my point here, but I did want to acknowledge that almost always there are more than just two options.) All the calculations around what we should do collectively need to be weighed against the current harms these systems are doing to people. And those harms are enormous. To be right, the things we advocate do not need to be perfect, just better than what we have.

But they have to *actually* be better. Not the reforms that increase state power and violence, like reentry courts and hate crime laws, but the things that *actually* keep us safe. Until then, disabled people—especially multiply marginalized ones—will be the ones paying the price. How much do you value our lives?

The Problem with Reform

We need to be critical of reforms, because the prison itself was seen as a reform of the less humane capital and corporal punishment they used in England. At first, prison was meant to be a time of rehabilitation, though as time went on the rehabilitative function of prisons has been completely abandoned, and now you can't even pretend prisons are supposed to be rehabilitative with a straight face.

People who are hesitant about abolition often say things like, "I don't know about abolition, but we definitely need reform." I understand why they say this, and I have likely said similar things in the past myself before I learned more about abolition. I point this out not to shame, but to unpack why advocating for reform instead of abolition is so harmful. (Shame is actually a tool that activists can and should thoughtfully use sometimes, but you'd know if I was trying to shame you!)

One problem is that "prison reform" doesn't actually mean anything. A reform is just a change, not necessarily positive or negative. Even if it is taken for granted that the changes are positive ones, positive according to whom? People of all political orientations, value systems, and knowledge levels talk about prison reform. The ends that many of them are working toward are the exact opposite of what I—and presumably you, if you're reading this book—want. For example, even the Koch brothers—rich assholes who funded conservative and Libertarian policies and politicians who came to prominence during the George W. Bush era—have an organization that works on "prison reform." Reform is just a change, and not all changes are helpful for us.

Mapping Abolition

No matter how much I want it to happen, prisons and police won't disappear tomorrow. Thought experiments about what it would be like if they did don't help anyone. Abolition is a process. One of the things that has helped the right gain so much power in the past few decades is that they know the world they are working toward and they have a destination they are moving toward together. Abolition can be our compass.

I sometimes use a map analogy to explain the importance of abolition instead of reform. For the purposes of this analogy, I'm going to use the examples of the US states of New York and California, which I chose only because they are far away from each other and most people have at least a vague idea where they are. Let's assume that the current system is New York, and that is where we are at the moment. Let's also assume that abolition—a society without prisons and police— is California. Everyone pretty much agrees that the current US criminal justice system is a mess. In terms of the analogy, we all want to leave New York. Abolitionists have a clear vision of where we want to go: California. However, reformers just want to leave New York but don't have a shared direction or even an end point at all. Reformists are just trying to get out of New York, and therefore they may go in any direction, including ones that make abolition less possible.

"Reform" isn't a destination, it just means you are moving. Though abolition and other ideologies may happen to over- lap on some policies, it's for totally different reasons. That's important, because the ends we are working toward may be different from those of reformers, because we have a specific place we are going. We have different destinations on the map. Just because we are moving doesn't mean we are going the right way.

Reform doesn't work when the roots and purpose of something are based on the control of marginalized bodies, especially Black and Indigenous ones. When something is rotten to its core, the only thing to do is destroy it. Anything else just allows the same imperialist and white supremacist systems to keep going, if perhaps more quietly. Abolition is the only answer.

Reformist Reforms versus Abolitionist Changes

One of the most important parts of learning about and applying concepts of abolition is understanding how to tell the difference between abolitionist changes and "reformist reforms." It's okay if it's not totally clear after just this section, because the following chapters contain many examples.

"Reformist reforms" sounds kind of redundant, and generally reforms are reformist (say that five times fast), but not always. So there needs to be a distinction between those that truly shrink carceral structures and those that don't.

As you probably could predict, abolitionist changes are things that bring us closer to a future without prisons, and reformist reforms are things that at first glance may seem helpful to an abolitionist goal but actually serve to strengthen and grow the carceral state. "Reformist reforms" is also the language that other abolitionists have used, so I want to keep it consistent, because I hope you are reading lots of other books about abolition.

I know that sometimes it looks like abolitionists can't celebrate our wins, but we have victories all the time. They just are often different ones. While I didn't feel celebratory during the 2021 US presidential inauguration, I did a month later when Illinois passed a law ending cash bail. I don't care about where you personally find joy; I'm focused on systems, not personal choices (though there are many things individuals can do to affect systems).

This is what many well-meaning people don't understand, and they dismiss abolitionists as not being willing to compromise. First of all, not compromising about life and death seems like something we should *all* aim for. That aside, just because something may seem like a good idea (e.g., body cameras and more police training) doesn't mean it actually makes things better, even in the ways it is intended to.

Sometimes people argue that it's better to do something than nothing, but that ignores a couple of important points. First, it assumes that the proposed intervention keeps the level of harm at the status quo or reduces harm, which the data does not back up. Whether through overt moving of resources or reinforcing myths (like the myth that "the police keep us safe"), reformist reforms increase the strength of carceral systems.

So-called prisoner reentry programs are a good example of a reformist reform. These programs differ, but the ones I've worked with focus on helping people who have recently been released get employment. Theoretically, this seems good, because having a criminal record makes it hard for people to find jobs, and these programs can help people. However, most of the employment that was acquired in these programs came from minimum-wage, unsustainable jobs that kept people in the same cycles of poverty that led to state involvement in the first place.

That doesn't mean there is no place for employment programs—jobs are important!—but there is so much more that people who are leaving prison need. Whether intentionally or not, reentry programs reinforce the idea that capitalism is the answer to criminalization, which isn't true theoretically or practically.

Beyond the way the concept of reentry doesn't contemplate the circumstances that led to incarceration, there are material costs. These programs demand resources from both the service providers and attendees—though the costs to attendees are rarely considered, even when they include having to pay actual money to the program—that would be better used to provide support. Beyond time and energy, there are even less tangible costs, such as the damage to self-esteem and shame. Of course, this stress leads to physical outcomes as well, all of which further disables people, making it even harder for them to get a job and thus be "successful" at reentry.

To go back to the map analogy, if you are in New York and trying to go to California, you wouldn't spend $500 on a ticket to Maine. Reentry programs, as they exist, are a good example of a reformist reform. (I say "as they exist" because there could—and should—be ways that recently freed people can connect to a community of abolitionists and access the other things they need.) But we can't get there if we keep going in the wrong direction. Many incarceration "alternatives" actually expand, reinforce, and legitimize carceral systems.

Beyond Prison and Police

Though abolition focuses on prisons and police, carceral systems include more than just jails and prisons. They also include psych wards, nursing homes, and institutions for the developmentally disabled. But it goes beyond that too. Part of the challenge of abolition is identifying the sneaky ways these systems coerce and oppress people, and the rest of this book focuses on how disabled people and communities are especially affected by carceral systems.

Foundational Sources

Anderson, William C. *The Nation on No Map: Black Anarchism and Abolition*. Chico, CA: AK Press, 2021.

Davis, Angela Y. *Are Prisons Obsolete?* New York: Seven Stories Press, 2003.

Gilmore, Ruth Wilson. *Golden Gulag: Prisons, Surplus, Crisis, and Opposition in Globalizing California*. Berkeley: University of California Press, 2007.

Kaba, Mariame. *We Do This 'til We Free Us: Abolitionist Organizing and Transforming Justice*. Chicago: Haymarket Books, 2021.

Kim, Alice, Erica R. Meiners, Audrey Petty, Jill Petty, Beth E. Richie, and Sarah Ross, eds. *The Long Term: Resisting Life Sentences, Working toward Freedom*. Chicago: Haymarket Books, 2018.

Law, Victoria. *"Prisons Make Us Safer" and 20 Other Myths about Mass Incarceration*. Boston: Beacon Press, 2021.

Levine, Judith, and Erica R. Meiners. *The Feminist and the Sex Offender: Confronting Sexual Harm, Ending State Violence*. London: Verso, 2020.

Ritchie, Andrea J. *Invisible No More: Police Violence against Black Women and Women of Color*. Boston: Beacon Press, 2017.

Schenwar, Maya, and Victoria Law. *Prison by Any Other Name: The Harmful Consequences of Popular Reforms*. New York: The New Press, 2020.

Vitale, Alex S. *The End of Policing*. London: Verso, 2018.

Disability Justice Concepts

Incarceration and disability are so intertwined that abolition is not possible without incorporating disability into our analysis. I focus on the history and principles of disability justice as a theory in the next chapter, but first we need to discuss some of the concepts that created the context for the disability justice movement.

What Is Disability?

When I use the term *disability* in this book (or *disabled people*) to refer to a category, I usually mean disability in its broadest sense, to mean any kind of "difference" that an individual or society considers to be an impairment. But disability also has other meanings. (For example, "disabled" also is a government status that may entitle someone to benefits with very specific and arduous requirements for proving eligibility.) Unless context makes it clear—or I specify otherwise—I use the broadest possible conception of disability, including physical disabilities, mental health disabilities, developmental disabilities, chronic illnesses, madness, D/deafness, blindness, neurodiversity, and on and on.

Someone may have a specific condition but not consider themselves "disabled." For example, some D/deaf people do not identify as disabled, though many others do. Disability is a political identity, but one that can only be assumed if you experience the world in a disabled body and/or mind. Disability is a personal and political identity whose meaning has changed over time. In this context, it is up to an individual to decide whether or not they identify as disabled.

All that said, this book is not generally concerned with how an individual identifies. If I limited my examination to people who have publicly said, "I am disabled," I wouldn't be able to make the connections I do. Even people who would be inclined to use that language may not have lived long enough to see the popularization of disability as an identity. Most people do not leave a record of how they identify. Therefore, I am using the information I have to make decisions about whether someone falls under the umbrella of disability to make larger points about the systems that exist.

Disability isn't just a concrete individual identity. It is also a concept that can be applied to systems even when there are not any disabled individuals around. I don't mean that disability is a metaphor; it's not. But the structures and institutions that undergird society have been created with a specific assumption of what disability is and how to "manage" it, and these paradigms have a direct impact on the material conditions of disabled people.

Most of the sources I rely on use different—usually vague—definitions of disability or a segment of disability. For example, a statistic will say "*x* percent of people with mental illness," but it doesn't specify what that means. Are these people who have been diagnosed with mental health disabilities? Just personality disorders? People who have been institutionalized? Does it include developmentally disabled people, who are either arbitrarily included or arbitrarily singled out under the "mental illness" umbrella?

All of this is just how we've decided to describe things, and we are free to change that at any time as we gather more information. Disability is not inherently bad, though it is universally oppressed, which can feel the same. Disability is not an insult or an inherently inferior way of being. I try to be as clear as possible with my definitions while also understanding disability as vast and fluid and impossible to get a hold of fully. I try to do the best I can using the information available, but there is so much we don't know—and so much these systems are designed to hide.

Models of Disability

There are a few different theories around disability that have heavily influenced how disabled people are treated. These theories are dynamic and flexible and can overlap at points. Understanding them is important, because how we conceptualize disability as a society determines how we treat disabled people.

Medical Model

The medical model is what is generally used in the US and is taken as a given; it believes in individual pathology, diagnosis, and cure. For example, let's say I have been feeling overwhelmed by hopelessness and fatigue. The assumption in the parts of the US that are white, educated, and middle class and have access to health insurance is that I contact some kind of health professional licensed by the state, maybe my primary doctor, maybe a psychiatrist, maybe a therapist. They may give me medications or recommend therapy, possibly allowing some other interventions depending on my health insurance. I'll likely get a diagnosis at some point in the process. But what all these methods have in common is that they are focused on individual change. Whether that change is biological (through medication) or behavior based (through therapy), even the most optimal end result in this paradigm leaves systems intact.

The medical model locates the problem of disability within the individual and sees disability as deviance from an able-bodied norm. This is directly tied to capitalism, and there's a neoliberal emphasis on the individual, in that the problem—and thus the solution—is seen as something within one's control.

This doesn't mean that therapy and medications and other things that use a medical model are useless; that's the only way to get any kind of care. It doesn't even mean the medical model is "bad" necessarily (though it has caused a lot of harm). "Medical model" isn't pejorative, it's a specific paradigm with a concrete viewpoint. Under a medical model worldview, disabled people are seen as problems to be fixed.

Diagnosis and the Medical Model

One feature of the medical model is the centrality of "diagnosis." By diagnosis I don't mean the process of figuring out why someone is experiencing a certain symptom, but the medical model concept that anything seen as deviating from the norm is a problem within an individual that should be named and "solved."

Diagnoses are culturally constructed categories that can change over time. For example, take the *Diagnostic and Statistical Manual of Mental Disorders* (DSM), a large book of all the classifiable "mental illnesses" compiled by the American Psychiatric Association. The most recent version, the DSM-5, is different in many ways from previous editions; it includes "disorders" that haven't been included before and removes others. My point being: like laws, diagnoses are ever changing and culturally contextual.

Diagnosis in itself isn't bad. Diagnosis in its broad form is just putting a word to something that someone is experiencing. Without the process of diagnosis, we wouldn't have medicine, which has saved so many lives. Diagnosis can be a key to finding the right treatment, but there is also the flip side of diagnosis, where these labels become an albatross that someone carries around and leads to stigma and criminalization.

Even the concept of diagnosis isn't as straightforward as it may seem. Diagnosis is also a heavily raced concept. Black men were (and still are) diagnosed with schizophrenia at rates much higher than other races, and the diagnosis was used tactically to disrupt Black liberation movements.[1] Diagnosis is always political.

Lack of Diagnosis

Lack of diagnosis is also political. In *Decarcerating Disability*, Liat Ben-Moshe explains:

> For many people of color or those who have no access to quality medical care, not being diagnosed is due less to viewing disability as a source of pride or as a fluid state and more to disparities in service provision and the ability to access doctors and medical services, such as therapy, medication, and early detection, because of inequalities based on class, color, language, or geographical barriers.[2]

Ben-Moshe makes an important point here that we also see in different contexts. While overdiagnosis is a problem, and diagnoses are stigmatized, for many multiply marginalized people it's the lack of (accurate) diagnosis that may be the more pressing problem. These two things are not in conflict with each other. Overdiagnosis and lack of diagnosis are both caused by negligent or absent medical care. They are two sides of the same coin.

Social Model

In contrast to the medical model, the social model locates the "problem" in the environment: it says that disabled people are not the issue, but rather things that interfere with access are the issue. Using the example above, the social model would say that there is nothing wrong with feeling hopeless and fatigued and that the problem is an environment that doesn't accommodate that. For example, if fatigue is keeping me from making it to my job on time, the social model would identify the problem as the requirement to get to work at a certain time and would suggest creating a work schedule that starts later in the day. The social model understands that there's nothing inherently wrong with fatigue or other markers of disability. While this is true, those of us with chronic illness and other disabilities sometimes do want treatments, and we may even want to be "cured."

Alison Kafer addresses this tension in *Feminist Queer Crip*:

> The social model with its impairment/disability distinction erases the lived realities of impairment; in its well-intentioned focus on the disabling effects of society, it overlooks the often-disabling effects of our bodies. People with chronic illness, pain, and fatigue have been among the most critical of this aspect of the social model, rightly noting that social and structural changes will do little to make one's joints stop aching or alleviate back pain.[3]

The social model focuses on the environment outside the person, but it does so in a problem-specific way that reacts to disability. However, while the social model looks at the environment, it tends to define "environment" narrowly and typically ignores the way oppressive systems play out in society.

Disability Rights Model

In the last chapter, I talked about a "both/and" approach to abolition. Using this approach, we can look at how some disability rights "achievements" of the past unintentionally strengthened the carceral system, while at the same time we can celebrate the gains that were made for (some) disabled people and the disability activists who got us here. However, and as will be discussed in greater detail later, there has been abolitionist work done under the "disability rights" banner, with deinstitutionalization being a notable example. So we can't just look at what something is called; we need to examine it more closely.

The disability rights model attempts to get disabled people the same amount of state power they would have if they were not disabled. In other words, it doesn't challenge the fundamental structure of the state or acknowledge marginalization aside from disability. It also is explicitly capitalist. As I'm writing this, the disability rights community in the US is celebrating the thirtieth anniversary of the passage of the Americans with Disabilities Act (ADA). The ADA is an important piece of United States legislation related to disability rights. The law and its amendments and regulations are expansive enough that I took a whole class on just the ADA in law school, so I'm focusing on one small part here to illustrate my point. I want to be clear that my critique comes from love and respect for the disabled people who got us here and is in service of achieving the dreams of liberation we all share.

The ADA was passed in 1990 under President George H.W. Bush. Title I of the ADA focuses on employment discrimination against people with disabilities (Section 12112). You're likely familiar with this part, as it's the one that requires covered employers to provide "reasonable accommodations" for disabled employees. This section has been incredibly helpful for disabled workers, and I use it all the time in my advocacy work.

But there are a few problems. First, according to the US Bureau of Labor Statistics, in 2022, the employment rate for disabled people in the US was 21.3 percent.[4] So for the vast majority of disabled people, this provision doesn't help them. Not every part of every law is for everyone, but it's not a random mix of disabled people who aren't protected. The ADA is most helpful for more privileged disabled people, because it doesn't include those who are "too disabled" to work.

All of this comes on top of the fact that multiply marginalized people with disabilities will still face disability discrimination along with whatever other employment discrimination they will encounter. Antidiscrimination legislation in the US doesn't contemplate intersectional identities, so people with multiple marginalizations have a harder time proving discrimination in court. (This is exactly the problem that caused Kimberlé Crenshaw to coin the term *intersectionality* in 1989.) The ADA's focus on disabled employment as the solution to disability discrimination ended up reinforcing capitalism, which values people based on their market output.

Meanwhile, many disability benefits require disabled people to live in abject poverty to receive them. By reinforcing the capitalist system and work as the ultimate purpose of a life, it devalued the lives of those of us who don't work in a capitalist sense.

Abolition understands that it's not a betrayal to the people who came before to be critical of their important work, because that is how we move forward. We can be piercing in our systemic analysis while also being gentle with each other. In many ways, disability justice is a marginalized response to the disability rights movement in the US. It's important to understand the difference between disability rights and disability justice approaches, because they mirror and overlap with the difference between strengthening the carceral state and abolition.

Disability Rights versus Disability Justice

While disability rights is about getting disabled people a piece of state power through achieving equality with nondisabled people, disability justice wants to dismantle the state and its power. Disability justice also rejects the idea of the disabled body (including the mind) as an imperfect version of a normative nondisabled body. In other words, there is no "default" body or mind that disabled people deviate from; bodies just come in all sorts of ways, which applies across identities. At the same time, disability justice acknowledges that the state does treat disabled and other marginalized people differently than nondisabled people, and multiply marginalized disabled people face the most state violence.

Sins Invalid—a disabled performance collective who I discuss at length in the next chapter—explains the difference as:

> At its core, the disability rights framework centers people who can achieve status, power, and access

through a legal or rights based framework, which we know is not possible for many disabled people, or appropriate for all situations.

The political strategy of the Disability Rights Movement relied on litigation and the establishment of a disability bureaucratic sector at the expense of developing a broad-based popular movement. Popular movements often begin when people develop political consciousness and name their experiences. Rights-based strategies often address the symptoms of inequity but not the root. The root of disability oppression is ableism and we must work to understand it, combat it, and create alternative practices rooted in justice.[5]

Disability justice is a great analysis to apply to abolition, because they are both born out of the same vision of liberation for all. For example, leadership of the most impacted requires that we center Black, disabled, and trans and nonbinary leadership, the people who are most harmed by policing and prisons. Disability justice also includes collective liberation, which of course includes everyone locked up in jails and prisons, but it also includes people in psych wards, institutions, and nursing homes, and even the people whose imprisonment is less visible, such as people under conservatorships and guardianships.

Changing the Paradigm

Disability justice is also a good jumping-off point to go beyond the concrete concepts and toward a dynamic understanding of the possibilities that can be applied personally and politically. One of my favorite illustrations of this concept is Ellen Samuels's "Six Ways of Looking at Crip Time":

> *Crip time is broken time.* It requires us to break in our bodies and minds to new rhythms, new patterns of thinking and feeling and moving through the world. It

forces us to take breaks, even when we don't want to, even when we want to keep going, to move ahead. It insists that we listen to our bodyminds *so* closely, *so* attentively, in a culture that tells us to divide the two and push the body away from us while also pushing it beyond its limits. Crip time means listening to the broken languages of our bodies, translating them, honoring their words.[6]

"Crip time" encompasses both theoretical and practical ways of being in the world. It centers the body instead of measuring time by the earth's relationship to the sun. It also accounts for the way that inaccessibility steals time. For example, it's common for wheelchair users to have to call several rideshare services or wait for the next bus because the driver took off when they saw that the person was disabled.

Samuels quotes friend Alison Kafer, explaining that "rather than bend disabled bodies and minds to meet the clock, crip time bends the clock to meet disabled bodies and minds."[7] Though Samuels doesn't explicitly name disability justice, this excerpt illustrates the way that unlike a rights model and like abolition, disability justice requires a whole shift in perspective and thinking.

Disability as a Racialized Concept

Disability is a racialized concept. Marginalized races, ethnicities, and cultures are all criminalized in different ways and have different relationships to disability. With that in mind, I focus here on just a couple of examples of the way that disability relates specifically to Blackness in the US. The relationship between Blackness and disability is especially important to investigate, because it explains so much about how we ended up where we are.

Just like prisons and policing are related to slavery, so is the way we think about disability. In an interview on the podcast *Groundings*, Dustin Gibson explains the connection between disability and slavery. Gibson discusses the 1840 census, which was the first time there were questions about both disability and race:

> That census says that the majority of free Black people were "insane" and "idiotic," to use their language, while saying that the majority of people that were still enslaved were sane. So it's creating this idea that to be free and Black, and to have the urge to want to be free and Black, is deemed to be a mental illness.[8]

There was even a medical diagnosis for slaves who had the overwhelming urge to run away: drapetomania. This shows that medicalization has always been a tool of white supremacy in the United States.

In their article "Work in the Intersections: A Black Feminist Disability Framework," Moya Bailey and Izetta Autumn Mobley explain the relationship between Blackness and disability:

> Race—and specifically Blackness—has been used to mark disability, while disability has inherently "Blackened" those perceived as unfit. Black people were—and continue to be—assumed intellectually disabled precisely because of race.[9]

In other words, white supremacy means that Black bodies are seen as inherently disabled, and disability is inherently bad. Ableism and racism are often used as pretexts for each other, which is why it's so important that we use the intersectional approach that disability justice calls for.

This legacy continues today. The incarceration rate for Black people is currently five times the incarceration rate for white people in state prisons. This is a pattern that continues across carceral locations. Racialized disabled people, but especially Black disabled people, must always be at the center of analyses, just as they're at the center of the state's crosshairs.

I cannot stress enough the importance of *adding* disability to an analysis that centers anti-Blackness and other targeted races and identities. The concept of "both/and" that I talked about in the last chapter means that we *add* the insights that a disability justice analysis gives; we are not substituting disability for Blackness or any other marginalized race or identity.

The following chapters include many examples of the way people living in a disabled, racialized body are targeted. Prisons and policing provide the scaffolding that lets white supremacy and ableism prop each other up.

Foundational Sources

Clare, Eli. *Brilliant Imperfection: Grappling with Cure*. Durham, NC: Duke University Press, 2017.

Clare, Eli. *Exile and Pride: Disability, Queerness, and Liberation*. Cambridge, MA: South End Press, 1999.

Kafer, Alison. *Feminist Queer Crip*. Bloomington: Indiana University Press, 2013.

Russell, Marta. *Capitalism and Disability*. Edited by Keith Rosenthal. Chicago: Haymarket Books, 2019.

History and Principles of Disability Justice

Disability justice is a way of looking at the world that centers disabled and marginalized wisdom and ways of being. It is also a concrete movement with a specific history and defined principles.

The Origins of Disability Justice

One of the foundational texts of disability justice is *Skin, Tooth, and Bone: The Basis of Movement Is Our People; A Disability Justice Primer* by Sins Invalid, a queer- and people-of-color-led disability performance project. According to the book, in 2005 disabled queers and activists of color started talking about a "second wave" of disability rights that went beyond the "rights" framework.[1]

These conversations were part of the backdrop that inspired the birth of Sins Invalid in 2006. Sins Invalid was started by Patty Berne, a disabled Japanese-Haitian queer nonbinary artist-activist, and Leroy F. Moore Jr., a disabled Black poet, community historian, artist-activist, and the founder of the Krip-Hop Nation. Over food and discussions of the sexual marginalization of disabled bodies, Patty and Leroy decided to create a performance project in which disabled bodies were celebrated.

Though they initially intended for the project to be a small-scale, one-time event, when they sent out a call for performers the response was so great that they knew they had tapped into a deep need for community and recognition.

Shayda Kafai documents the history of Sins Invalid in *Crip Kinship: The Disability Justice and Art Activism of Sins Invalid*:

"By 2008, two years after what was meant to be a onetime performance, Sins Invalid officially became a performance project grown out of need and in solidarity with crip family and love."[2]

Sins Invalid continues to grow and create meaningful work centered around racialized, disabled, queer bodies. As their work caught on, however, they saw the term *disability justice* begin to be used in ways they did not support. Kafai explains:

> In 2015, Patty (Berne) began to notice that people were using Disability Justice outside of its disabled, queer of color origins.... Patty also noticed that the framework was being misused and co-opted primarily by white academics and activists who were using disability justice as a framework, while the community who created it, the communities that it was meant to sustain and support, had not had a chance to define its parameters. These occurrences pushed Patty, Sins Invalid's artist-activists, and fellow disabled, queer, and trans of color communities to establish a written record and a cohesive definition of Disability Justice.[3]

Berne ended up with a list of ten principles.

Ten Principles of Disability Justice

The ten principles that Berne identified are: intersectionality, leadership of the most impacted, anticapitalism, cross-movement organizing, wholeness, sustainability, cross-disability solidarity, interdependence, collective access, and collective liberation. While they are relatively self-explanatory, I think it will be helpful to look at each one a little closer.

Intersectionality

Intersectionality is based in concepts of Black feminism and womanism, such as those put forth by the Combahee River

Collective in their seminal 1977 statement.[4] Black women, who face both sexism and racism, were often unable to prove their cases for these in court, because discrimination against Black women didn't fit neatly into discrimination law, as the laws were written as if someone could only be discriminated against based on one characteristic. This problem inspired Kimberlé Crenshaw to coin the term *intersectionality*.[5] More recently, Moya Bailey created the term *misogynoir* to describe the unique sexism and racism Black women are forced to endure.[6]

Since the term *intersectionality* was originally created, it has moved away from the legal field and into mainstream discourse. It's not always clear what people mean when they talk about intersectionality, so let me tell you what I mean when I use it. I'm referring to the way identities intersect and overlap, but I also mean the way these identities become more than the sum of their parts. In other words, marginalizations don't add up, they multiply.

TL Lewis is a community attorney and organizer who focuses on making links between ableism, racism, and other forms of oppression. Lewis's work also includes cofounding Helping Educate to Advance the Rights of Deaf communities (HEARD), a cross-disability abolitionist organization. Lewis writes:

> When a Black Disabled person is killed by the state, media and prominent racial justice activists usually report that a Black person was killed by the police. Contemporaneous reports from disability rights communities regarding the very same individual usually emphasize that a Disabled or Deaf Individual was killed by the police—with not one word about that person's race, ethnicity or indigenous roots. . . .
>
> To be sure, disability and deaf communities of color are disproportionately impacted by state violence. Even still, most resourced disability rights organizations

refuse to take action to end the crisis of racialized people with disabilities dying in our schools, streets, homes and prisons; whilst resourced non-disability civil rights entities dishonor the lives of the same people by failing to uplift their whole humanity. This, even when these resourced entities claim to be fighting for justice "in their name."[7]

The point isn't to use disability to replace race (or other categories) but to also include disability in an analysis that not only includes race, gender, and so on but actively puts marginalized identities at the center of the analysis (that is, "both/and"). One example is abortion. Even if abortion is legal, if it costs too much for someone to access it, they can't get the benefit of it. So one way that intersectionality can be applied in reproductive rights is not only to fight for legality but to fight as hard for abortion to be free or covered by the state. (Some states actually do cover it through their Medicaid, but due to the Hyde Amendment no state can use federal money, which is fucked up.)[8]

Intersectionality requires not just thinking about the barriers the most privileged people face—in this example, legality—but also the barriers less privileged people confront, like the ability to pay. Intersectionality means centering the liberation of those living at the margins of the margins.

Leadership of the Most Impacted

Disability justice understands that lived experience— particularly for those of us with multiply marginalized identities—gives us important and unique insight that needs to be honored. In other words, disability justice centers the exact people the rights approach ignores: those with the least access to state power. Even beyond the moral aspect of focusing on those suffering most under the current system, it makes sense strategically. Lived experience gives people an expertise that can't be gained any other way, and things that protect everyone will always be better than things that protect only some people. When it comes to reducing oppression, a rising tide lifts all boats. Using the needs of those most impacted by systems as our guideposts will help everyone.

Anticapitalism

Capitalism is inherently ableist, because it privileges the body's ability to produce above everything else, including the survival of the species as a whole. The gears of capitalism have no problem grinding up disabled bodies, both figuratively and literally. Thus, disability justice is incompatible with capitalism.

The relationship between capitalism and disability is more complicated than it may seem at first. Disabled people don't just participate in capitalism through labor and consumption but also as commodities that can make money for companies through their incarceration, as with group homes and nursing homes. Disabled people aren't just subjects of capitalism, we are also objects.

Cross-Movement Organizing

Since disability justice is an intersectional movement, we also must commit to cross-movement organizing. Cross-movement organizing means working with other marginalized communities to build collective power. It's what I am trying to do here with disability justice and abolition movements.

Wholeness

Disabled people are often not treated as actual people. Even when we are, it sometimes seems more that we've been rounded up to "person" by someone nondisabled because they are feeling nice that day and grading on a curve rather than because they actually see us as complete and unique people. Boiled down, wholeness is as simple as recognizing that disabled people are actual people with thoughts, feelings, personalities, and, for many of us, sexual fantasies and practices. I have an unfinished poem somewhere about how fucking horrible things must be for us that even recognizing disabled people as fully human has to be one of our demands.

This isn't unique to the disabled community, of course. Black Lives Matter simply requests that non-Black people acknowledge the humanity of Black people, and even that is pushed back against, especially by white people. One of the ways that oppression is furthered is through dehumanization of the "other."

Sustainability

We can't just use disability justice to articulate our political goals; we also need to include it in the fabric of how our movements are built. The way our movements are currently constructed leads to so much burnout. Though Leah Lakshmi Piepzna-Samarasinha wrote this about transformative justice specifically, it's also true of the abolition movement in general:

> We need to take a breath and dare to imagine models for doing this work that are actually sustainable. This could look like planning for breaks, having different roles for folks, allowing folks who have been doing the work for years to move into mentorship and advisor roles, or just understanding that the only way to do [abolition] isn't to hold fifteen intense processes at once. Instead of being surprised by crises, collapse, and triggers, what if we planned for them? And most of all: What would our (abolitionist) work look like if we put everyone's needs at the center?[9]

Movements need to be sustainable to work. While the unsustainability of the current status quo disproportionately impacts disabled people, even nondisabled people burn out. We all have bodies, and all bodies have needs.

Cross-Disability Solidarity

We can't throw some disabled people under the bus for the sake of others. For example, sometimes people with physical disabilities may make a point of stressing their "mental fitness" (and vice versa). This stigmatizes some disabilities and reinforces ableist norms as a whole.

In "Changing the Framework," Mia Mingus writes:

> Disability is not monolithic. Ableism plays out differently for wheelchair users, deaf people or people who have mental, psychiatric and cognitive disabilities. None of these are mutually exclusive, and all are complicated by race, class, gender, immigration, sexuality, welfare status, incarceration, age and geographic location.[10]

Disability justice is about the liberation of *all* disabled people. Sins Invalid explained both the importance of mixed ability organizing and its practical challenges:

> Mixed ability organizing requires us to identify and bridge between different capacities, orientations, and relationships to power. It means paying attention to and being honest about the complexities of being in a body, and developing practices capable of attending to that complexity. For instance, while people with different disabilities may share a common experience of oppression under ableism, it can also be true that particular contexts can provide for the access needs of some and not others. A particular meeting space may present difficulties for people with mobility impairments, while a particular style of conducting a meeting may be difficult for people with emotional or cognitive impairments. These complexities play out not only across disabilities, but across race, gender, sexuality, class, and so on. For mixed ability organizing to honor the principles of

disability justice, it must take stock of, engage with, and work through these complexities.[11]

The process of figuring this out is an organic opportunity to develop cohesion. If done properly, it can bond a group better than those training exercises that I hate (but acknowledge do have a purpose sometimes). From the beginning, you are reinforcing the norm of not leaving anyone behind.

Interdependence

The centering of interdependence in disability justice is a direct challenge to capitalism and the carceral state. Sins Invalid rejects the white supremacist value of independence and puts it in a historical context:

> Before the massive colonial project of Western European expansion, we understood the nature of interdependence within our communities. We see the liberation of all living systems and the land as integral to the liberation of our own communities, as we all share one planet. We work to meet each other's needs as we build toward liberation, without always reaching for state solutions which inevitably extend state control further into our lives.[12]

Interdependence acknowledges that we all need each other, and that is a good thing. Caring for each other in all of the ways we do (including fighting for justice) is an opportunity for liberation, not a burden.

Collective Access

Collective access allows everyone to be at the metaphorical table. If disabled (and other marginalized) people can't be there—besides being inherently unjust—an abled worldview will almost definitely be centered. In the same essay quoted above, Mia Mingus wrote about the importance of accessibility for everyone:

Our communities and movements must address the issue of access. There is no way around it. Accessibility is concrete resistance to the isolation of disabled people. Accessibility is nothing new, and we can work to understand access in a broad way, encompassing class, language, childcare, gender-neutral bathrooms as a start.

We must, however, move beyond access by itself. We cannot allow the liberation of disabled people to be boiled down to logistics. We must understand and practice an accessibility that moves us closer to justice, not just the inclusion of diversity.[13]

Accessibility is crucial, but it's just the beginning. Accessibility isn't just about allowing disabled people in, it's about the changes that happen when disabled people are involved. Accessibility isn't charity, it's a way to strengthen our movements and be more effective. Access is necessary—but not sufficient!—for disability justice.

Collective Liberation

This brings us, finally, to collective liberation. Disability justice understands that liberation must include everyone. While a disability rights approach is one that is focused on asking the current system to include more rights and protections for disabled people, a disability justice approach understands that the systems themselves are the problem. The difference between abolition and reform can sometimes mirror the difference between disability justice and disability rights.

Disability Justice Requires Abolition

Both disability justice and abolition share the idea that no one is disposable. To abolish prisons, we need to center disability, and to work toward disability justice, we need to abolish police and prisons.

Liat Ben-Moshe explains it this way:

> The call for connecting analysis of incarceration and
> decarceration with disability is also a call to pay atten-
> tion to the lives of mostly poor people of color who are
> incarcerated worldwide, in prisons, detention centers,
> nursing homes, or institutions for those with labels of
> "mental illness" and/or "intellectual disability." . . . Race
> is coded in disability, and vice versa. It's impossible to
> untangle antiblack racism from processes of pathologi-
> zation, ableism, and sanism.[14]

Disability justice is not compatible with a reform approach
that continues to target and cage disabled people. Disability
justice requires abolition.

The chapters that follow address some of what this means
for disabled people and abolitionist activism. It's crucial for
abolitionists to sharpen their analysis around disability justice
and for those interested in disability justice to understand
abolition.

Foundational Sources

Kafai, Shayda. *Crip Kinship: The Disability Justice and Art Activism of
   Sins Invalid*. Vancouver: Arsenal Pulp Press, 2021.

Samuels, Ellen. "Six Ways of Looking at Crip Time." *Disability Studies
   Quarterly* 37, no. 3 (2017). https://doi.org/10.18061/dsq.v37i3.

Sins Invalid. *Skin, Tooth, and Bone: The Basis of Movement Is Our People;
   A Disability Justice Primer*. 2nd ed. Berkeley, CA: Sins Invalid, 2019.

Sex Work, Disability, and Criminalization

All of these ideas can seem abstract, so I wanted to take a closer look at one of the ways these systems can come together. I'm going to use an example from my own life while also connecting it to broader structures. I want to talk about the relationship between sex work, disability, and criminalization.

Sex work is a term coined in 1979 by Carol Leigh—a legendary sex work activist—to refer to the jobs that make up the sex industry, including escorting, stripping, porn, camming, and phone sex.[1] There are huge differences between different aspects of sex work and how much they are criminalized. Though it's unspecific, the term can still be useful, because the reality of the industry is that it's very common to work in different aspects of it over time or simultaneously. Also, the lawyer side of me likes that we can use this term to talk about these things without anyone needing to openly admit to anything illegal.

I started doing sex work after I got too sick to keep working in my job as a lawyer. I needed a job that I could do when I am able—and one that I could take months off from at a time, as my autoimmune illness flares sometimes require. While I do have a partner who is employed, we have four kids, and being sick is expensive, so I couldn't afford my medication without bringing in some kind of income. Obviously, this would not be everyone's choice, and there is much more context, but that is more appropriate for a memoir, so I'm not getting much into my personal experiences here. But my five years (and counting!) in the industry have taught me so many things.

As I began meeting other people who worked in the sex industry, I realized that a lot of them had similar stories to mine: they got into sex work in part (or full) due to their disabilities. This seemed to be true across different sex industry jobs. There are many reasons for this, including that some kinds of sex work have a low barrier to entry. For many you don't need to have any specific qualifications, or be hired by a boss, or maintain consistent hours.

At the same time, certain parts of the industry are prohibitive to different bodies. For example, stripping is not accessible to a lot of people with physical disabilities. All of this said, there is disability representation in every single aspect of the sex industry. Though I don't get into it too much here, the way this provides nuance to narratives around desirability and disability is quite interesting.

As I made (and lived) this connection, I found that few people were talking about the relationship between disability and criminalized economies in general—and sex work specifically. While there are no specific numbers, once you look, it's inarguable that sex workers are disproportionately disabled.

But before I talk about the link between sex work and disability, I want to talk about the criminalization faced by sex workers, especially full-service sex workers.

Criminalization

Criminalization is the process of getting more people under the carceral umbrella by making certain activities illegal. Criminalization goes beyond just the potential criminal penalties an individual faces after an arrest, because the effects ripple outward. When "prostitution" is a crime—as it is in the vast majority of the US—in order to avoid arrest, sex workers have to do things that may be dangerous in other ways, such as meeting a client somewhere isolated to avoid police.

Juno Mac and Molly Smith explore this issue in *Revolting Prostitutes: The Fight for Sex Workers' Rights*:

Criminalization is a multi-pronged trap. Convictions, [broken windows policing], and prostitute [arrests] hinder sex workers' ability to secure other jobs and lead to accumulating debts for fines, pushing them into continuing to sell sex....

Criminalization pushes Mariana to work in ways that made her more vulnerable to the man who killed her. On the night of her murder, Mariana had been verbally admonished by the police three times and handed a caution. She needed to work to pay a soliciting fine she had received a few days earlier. (Another woman in the area at the same time had a fine totaling £1,350.) Her reasons for working later than normal and in a more secluded way are clear—she desperately needed to avoid the police, to make the money that she needed to avoid another expensive fine.[2]

Sex work is not inherently dangerous, but sex workers are at high risk of violence, in part because we tend to be multiply marginalized and therefore more vulnerable to state and interpersonal violence, for the reasons I explain in this book. The other thing that makes sex work so dangerous is criminalization. To avoid arrest, sex work has to remain underground, leading to much more isolation by sex workers, which makes victimization easier.

Sex Workers and Police

For sex workers, the police are nothing but dangerous. Even in the rare cases that sex workers try to go to police for help after violence, they are often refused. In *Playing the Whore: The Work of Sex Work*, Melissa Gira Grant discusses the relationship between sex workers and police:

Carol told researchers, "if I call [the police], they don't come. If I have a situation in the street, forget it. 'Nobody told you to be in the street.' After a girl was gang-raped they said, 'Forget it, she works in the street.'"[3]

When violence does happen, sex workers have no recourse. The police don't take violence against sex workers seriously, and victims involved in the sex trade can face arrest for reporting it. Oftentimes it is the police who are the perpetrators. Under the current structure, carceral state responses are the only option presented to deal with violence, but the carceral state only cares about certain kinds of violence against certain kinds of people.

It's not just those who work on the street who are vulnerable to police violence (though it would still be an issue if it was!). But Gira Grant notes that even "indoor" sex workers—who are generally more privileged—face police violence, including sexual assault:

> In a parallel survey conducted by the Sex Workers Project, 14 percent of those who primarily work indoors reported the police had been violent towards them; 16 percent reported that the police had initiated a sexual interaction.[4]

When people ask, "How do we stay safe without police?" all they need to do is look at sex workers. Sex workers are already living in a world where we cannot go to the police for help. When I first started doing sex work, there was a man who had been violently raping and beating sex workers for over a decade. The police refused to act for many years, even when sex workers had evidence and had essentially conducted the whole investigation themselves, to the point where workers would have his exact location. Sex workers tried for years to give this information to the police, and they didn't want it. After sex workers organized and pressured the police, he was eventually arrested in 2020.[5] In a press release, the New Jersey district attorney admitted that even though they knew he raped and assaulted sex workers, they only charged him with coercion and enticement. My point isn't that we need the police to arrest more people, but that they only "help" those they decide to. Sex work isn't inherently violent, but criminalization is.

Research on Disabled Sex Workers

Because sex workers are disproportionately disabled, sex work decriminalization and the safety of sex workers is a disability issue. However, we are a population that has been ignored. While there are definitely benefits to not having even more researchers sniffing around, in order to learn about disabled sex workers, I had to do my own research.

Though it hasn't been explored much formally, there is a ton of anecdotal and qualitative evidence of a relationship between disability and sex work (and more coming out all the time). I wanted to learn more about other disabled sex workers' experiences, so I sent out a questionnaire that about ten sex workers responded to, and I have anonymously included some of their perspectives below.

How Disability and Sex Work Are Related

One sex worker with fibromyalgia who answered my questions explained that with sex work she is "in control of my own schedule, so if I am having a flare, I can cancel everything and take care of my body the way I need without needing to report to a boss or just power through."

Another said:

> My disabilities have impacted my ability to work, especially in low-paying, labor-heavy work. Time and time again I would have to go on short-term disability, was replaced, had to quit, and was fired from various jobs because of this. I missed too much work because I was too sick. That equated to me being a terrible employee even if I was terrific on the days I was able to attend

work. This made me feel like a failure. I was too broken and I did not fit in this system.

It's important to understand that "being able to work" means more than just the physical ability to perform the job. A lot of us have mental health issues—myself included—that in part or in whole keep us from being able to work traditional jobs. For example, one person explained how other work brought on suicidal breakdowns:

> Long story short is that over a year's time of working full-time hours I was hospitalized three separate times for suicidal ideation/mental breakdowns. These experiences informed my decision to [do] sex work because I fundamentally do not have the constitution to endure working in secular work environments due to the flaring of symptoms of my disabilities.

Disability, Desirability, Visibility, Fetishization, and Sex Work

One of the biggest reasons the relationships between disability and sexuality generally and disability and sex work specifically are not talked about is that disabled people are constantly desexualized by society. The abstract idea that disabled people have sex is hard enough for some abled people to grasp, but that disabled people are being paid for being sexy is beyond what they can imagine.

For some folks, sex work has helped them to work through the desexualization they have internalized. One sex worker wrote: "As a sex worker, I feel more free to explore my sexual identity. As a disabled person, my sexual identity is largely erased. In a more transactional setting, I am acknowledged and appreciated as a desirable sexual being."

However, not all disabled people and disabilities are treated equally. It's still incredibly rare to see a *visibly* disabled person in porn, and when you do it's usually fetishized.

(Fetishization of disabled people is too huge and nuanced to get into now, but it is a relevant and important issue.) But that is starting to change a little bit and will hopefully continue to change. One disabled sex worker told me:

> Models with medical aids such as feeding tubes can still make good money. I was so fearful when I got my feeding tubes that no one would buy my content. I have literally been published and featured on sites since I started respecting my health and limits. It is so refreshing. My sales have actually doubled since I got my feeding tube, and I haven't been fetishized and am rarely even asked.

Being disabled does not necessarily prohibit someone from being a sex worker, and in my experience disability is the rule, not the exception. (Though there is still a ton of ableism in the sex industry, but that's a conversation for another time.)

Reformist Reforms versus Abolitionist Reforms: Sex Work Version
Decriminalization Not Legalization

The distinction between decriminalization and legalization is an important one, especially for disabled sex workers. Decriminalization is what sex workers want, which is a repeal of the laws that make "prostitution" illegal. Decriminalization gives sex workers a tiny bit more insulation from police.

The sex workers who responded to my questions lived in different states and countries, so there were different laws around the criminalization of sex work. However, those who lived where full-service sex work, what the state calls "prostitution," was illegal unanimously said it made their lives harder and more dangerous.

Legalization makes it so that prostitution is only decriminalized *for some people in some circumstances*. With legalization, some sex workers are allowed to operate legally, but not all of them, because it requires registration and complying with other state requirements. This keeps the underground sex trade flourishing, and studies show that legalization does not reduce sex trafficking like decriminalization does. Sex workers who aren't able to meet the regulatory requirements will still be criminalized. Sex workers with certain mental health, cognitive, and other disabilities may have a much more difficult time completing the requirements, still leaving disabled sex workers especially vulnerable to criminalization.

However, decriminalization of prostitution on its own is not enough. Even if sex work is decriminalized, sex workers are still in danger of being criminalized under other laws. Broken windows policing is a theory of policing where even small "quality of life" crimes are penalized, like drinking outside or possessing drugs or loitering. These laws being on the books allows for police to harass and criminalize sex workers still, just under different pretenses.

Disability organizers should understand that rampant discrimination means that disabled people are more likely to be part of criminalized economies, and thus they should make sure they have an intersectional understanding and not work with the police or other officials who may put disabled sex workers at risk. This also means that mainstream disability organizations need to include the needs of sex workers in their work and adopt an explicitly decriminalization policy position around sex work and a nonengagement policy with the police.

From working toward prison abolition to making a commitment to not call the police, there are many ways allies can support disabled sex workers. It's also important for the disability community to support sex workers and sex worker organizing to be accessible and center disability justice.

Get Rid of Human Trafficking Court

In New York State, there is something called a "human trafficking court" (HTC).[6] When someone is arrested for prostitution or a similar crime, judges may have the discretion to send them to the HTC. After completion of the court, the charges will be dismissed.

HTC is a liberal reform that has added to the criminalization and oppression that sex workers face. Even on its face, this "court" doesn't make sense. First of all, who is it for? If someone is a survivor of trafficking, why are you giving them criminal penalties so that they have to be involved in a court? If the court is meant to punish people who "traffic" others, why does completion result in charges being dropped? The court was created and has always been a way to punish multiply marginalized sex workers. Even calling it "human trafficking court" is intentional propaganda that conflates consensual adult sex work with human trafficking, which is dangerous for sex workers and trafficking survivors, two communities that have a ton of overlap and are overwhelmingly multiply marginalized people.

In *Revolting Prostitutes: The Fight for Sex Workers' Rights*, Juno Mac and Molly Smith point out that these courts treat actual trafficking survivors the same way they treat consensual adult sex workers. That means that "victims" of human trafficking get arrested too and end up in these courts. These supposedly "progressive" courts use the same approach that evangelical organizations do, making it much harder for trafficking survivors to actually come forward, because they will likely be arrested.

Once someone gets arrested and funneled into human trafficking court, they must comply with many requirements, which may include counseling, drug tests, and other costly and time-intensive interventions. If they fail one of these, they will likely end up back in jail with a longer sentence than they would have otherwise had without the trafficking court. Further, police are more likely to arrest people they know will end up in a trafficking court rather than a regular court, so an incident that in the past would end with someone being let go now will be more likely to end in an arrest for the sex worker's "own sake."

What Does All of This Mean?

If I didn't get sick, I probably wouldn't have ended up doing sex work. That's not a negative thing. Being sick is difficult, but sex work isn't bad as far as jobs go. So from both a political and personal perspective, I want to underscore that engagement in sex work is not a value judgment. Whether disabled people are overrepresented in sex work is not necessarily a good or bad thing in itself. But if disabled people feel like they are forced into sex work because they have no other way to support themselves, that is a problem. If sex work is damaging to our bodies, we should be able to respect those limits while having our basic needs met. However, for disabled people especially, sex work can help to create some of the care communities we need to survive, and these communities have ways to keep each other safe that don't involve cops.

What can we take from this? Well, to start, there are a lot of disabled people who are doing sex work because their disabilities keep them from working other jobs and disability benefits are unavailable or not enough to meet their needs. We fear criminalization, but we also feel like we don't have other options. The nature of the sex trade, the huge variety of sex work, and the low barrier to entry make it accessible to disabled people in a way that other jobs aren't. Sex work can also be extremely ableist, especially toward visibly disabled people. More than anything, it means that we have so much more to know and to do when it comes to supporting both sex workers and disabled people in this society.

Why Is This Important?

The purpose of all this isn't so that white, graduate-degreed, disabled sex workers like me can center ourselves in conversations about sex work, but to support the disabled sex workers who experience the most criminalization, especially those who are currently incarcerated in jails, prisons, hospitals, nursing homes, and elsewhere, which will inherently help us all. As Dean Spade talks about, rights don't trickle down, they trickle up.[7] Again, a rising tide of justice lifts all boats.

The narratives around sex workers and disabled people are both one-dimensional, and if you buy into all of them, you would think disabled sex workers don't exist. But we do. One respondent put it beautifully when they said, "People often have misconceptions of who sex workers are, and I encourage everyone to reevaluate their thoughts and take a good look at the world around them and how things are changing."

Foundational Sources

Gira Grant, Melissa. *Playing the Whore: The Work of Sex Work*. London: Verso, 2014.

Mac, Juno, and Molly Smith. *Revolting Prostitutes: The Fight for Sex Workers' Rights*. London: Verso, 2018.

Short-Term Care

Many carceral systems exist under the guise of "caring" for disabled people, and care is often at least part of the rationale for their continued existence. However, these places do not provide care in any kind of real or humane way—in large part because their purpose was never actually to care for disabled people.

Since I needed to divide this subject up somehow, I split it into "long-term care" and "short-term care," but this is a false binary, as the two are inherently intertwined and bleed into each other. By short-term care I generally mean responses to acute crises, such as hospital psych wards, detoxes, and jails, while in the long-term care chapter I discuss institutions, nursing homes, and other places where disabled people are supposed to spend the rest of their lives locked up.

Everyone needs care, though some care is more socially acceptable to need than others. Disabled people take issue with the term *special needs*, because everyone has needs. For example, we all need to be taught things and we all have different ways of learning, but in public school, whether or not your "needs" are considered normative depends on the standards set by the schools. All of these standards are arbitrary and/or come from the long history of colonization, ableism, and white supremacy that has formed our current understandings of who deserves care and in what ways they deserve it.

I detail throughout the next sections the problem with settling for our current system of "care," especially where disabled people are concerned. I also explore some of the practices that have been tried and other ideas for creating the noncarceral care that is needed. You'll notice many repeating themes between officially carceral institutions like jails and prisons and the places disabled people are locked up "for our own good."

Dealing with Crisis

One of the common questions I am asked about abolishing the police is what will happen to people who are in crisis—usually they mean mental health crisis—if there is no police. Before I get into my answer, I want to reflect on the question itself for a minute. I can't help but notice that often (but not always) the question is framed in a way that makes clear that the questioner is not asking, "What will happen to me if I am in crisis?" but instead wondering, "Who will keep the crazy people away from me?"

In a way, this is understandable. We have been taught that there is some "other" inherently dangerous group of "mentally ill" people that we need to keep ourselves and our communities safe from. (This is usually racialized too, of course.) But the disabled people who the police are using these violent tactics on are not "them" but "us": your mom with depression, your child with schizophrenia, you after a future crisis.

One thing that makes disability unique is that any of us can become disabled at any time. We need to make sure we are thinking about these policies from the perspective of the safety of the most vulnerable person in the situation.

This isn't a judgment on the knee-jerk reaction that has been culturally embedded in us. It's a call to interrogate those reactions and to not make decisions based on feelings but instead on the actual impacts. To borrow from Mariame Kaba: I don't care about your fucking feelings. I care what you are fighting for.

It's important to understand that people with disabilities—including psychiatric disabilities—aren't any more dangerous than nondisabled people.[1] In fact, disabled people are three times more likely than nondisabled people to experience serious violence.[2] Even if someone is having a severe mental health crisis, the major concern in the situation is much more likely to be suicide than homicide. You don't need to be protected from disabled people; disabled people are the ones who need protection.

Also, not everyone with visible mental health disabilities is in crisis. Ableism tells us that to have any kind of disability is to suffer a horrible fate, when the vast majority of the negative consequences of being disabled come from society rather than from the disability itself. It is true that sometimes people are in crisis and need support, but police and other carceral interventions are not the answer, and they tend to make things worse. We need to build noncarceral services that are actually safe for people in crisis, whether from mental health issues or another emergency.

Finally, if we are in crisis, you should treat us like everyone else and help us if you have the capacity and ability to do so—like you would anyone else. Disabled people aren't some separate species. We need housing and food and health care just like everyone else. If we are lacking necessary care, then the solution should be to get us care, not involve people who greatly increase the risk of violence.

The Police Make Things Worse

People with mental health and psychiatric disabilities are in special danger from police and are consistently targeted for arrest because the disabilities themselves are criminalized. Exhibiting symptoms of mental illness in public is enough to get someone arrested. One of the many reasons that people without homes are especially at risk of being arrested is because of the inability to have their symptoms in private. In most places, the police are the entity designated to respond to mental health emergencies, and we have been conditioned to think that they will help the situation. However, the police can only make things worse.

The police don't defuse situations, they escalate them. The only thing they are capable of doing—aside from committing overt violence—is arresting someone or bringing them to the emergency room. That's literally it. Well-meaning people sometimes call the police because they want to get someone "help," but often the reason the person is in crisis in the first place is because of the lack of health care, and calling the police just puts them in a position where it's even harder to get care. In other words, the problem is not solved with police, it's solved with resources.

Dealing with Violence without Police

Even though it's a myth that disabled people are more violent than nondisabled people, sometimes there are situations that are potentially violent even in the absence of police. As one of the founders of a Canadian antipsychiatry group that ran a house for people in mental health crisis founded on noncoercive principles, Gisela Sartori has on-the-ground experience:

> People ask, what if someone comes in who's really angry and wants to hit people? Our answer is that we will give them lots of things they can hit. We'll tell them they can hit things and throw things against the walls in this room, but that they can't hit people.
>
> In four years of existence, no one has ever been violent at SOS [Second Opinion Society]. Once, someone came after me with a butcher knife. And I said, very clearly and calmly, "Put that knife down." And that was it.[3]

Situations like this sound (and can be!) very scary, especially if you don't have experience with this stuff. However, most of the people I know who have spent time either on the streets or in direct service would be able to handle a situation like this in a way that deescalates the situation and leads to greater safety for everyone.

Not so the police.

Here's the thing: Police are cowards. They are scared, which is why they need so many weapons. They are encouraged to see other community members as "the enemy" instead of partners in creating safety, which makes them paranoid and unable to accurately gauge actual threats to community safety. Police usually escalate situations, and no amount of training will change that, because of the fundamental nature of policing.

When the police are called, the absolute best-case scenario is that they act as a taxi to take someone to get "help" without arrest or injury (but inevitably with trauma). In the US, this almost always means the emergency room (ER), which has itself become criminalized.

The Emergency Room Is a Criminalized Space

Like a terrible lottery, each trip to the ER increases someone's chances for law enforcement contact. Many hospitals have their own police or employ local police or security. That the place where people go when symptoms may be flaring is also somewhere that is under constant police surveillance is a terrible combination.

The ER has become the catchall place for acute care, especially for those without health insurance. Like other places that primarily serve marginalized people, the ER is criminalized. In a June 2021 issue of the *Harvard Law Review*, Ji Seon Song wrote a lengthy article about the way that contact with the ER can lead to incarceration:

> Sociologists have described how police monitor those who come to hospitals and emergency rooms and how nurses in a public emergency room allocate medical care based on perceptions of patients' criminality. Hospital professionals have observed officers

jotting down patient names and birthdates even when they were not in police custody. Doctors in an urban hospital witnessed security routinely handing over patient cell phones to police, also when they were not in police custody. At yet another hospital, the sheriff's office providing security installed license plate readers at the ER entrance without the hospital's knowledge. Police execute warrants and make arrests in hospitals. Police ask doctors and nurses about injuries and diagnoses. They stand watch during procedures. Meanwhile, doctors, nurses, and other hospital staff become part of police investigations. Beyond helping police by performing procedures and testing, they pass on information about patients. They direct police officers to patients and attest to their capabilities for questioning.[4]

Because of the lack of public health care in the US, many poor people—who are disproportionately disabled—are forced to go to the ER to get any kind of treatment. This is because there is a federal law that requires emergency rooms to stabilize and treat anyone in medical crisis whether or not they are insured or can pay.[5]

Since disabled people will disproportionately require medical care, we are also disproportionately affected by the criminalization of the ER. Poor disabled people of color are especially at risk of being arrested, which is not only unjust but also adds yet another barrier to accessing healing. Song makes the important point that "by coming into a hospital, patients assume the risk that they will be subject to police surveillance, search, and questioning. The cost of obtaining medical care is police access."[6]

Accessing care in the ER necessarily means being surveilled during the notoriously long time that you usually have to spend in the waiting room. Since people with private health insurance can usually get care outside of the ER—including preventative care that reduces the need for the ER—as usual the surveillance burden and therefore risk of arrest is on the most marginalized. Disabled people are not more "criminal" than other people, they are just surveilled more.

Suicide Prevention

A huge part of emergency mental health is suicide prevention, but suicide prevention cannot be relegated to only emergencies. It needs to be part of the fabric of everything we do. In other words, part of suicide prevention is making sure that people have enough money to live comfortably, have housing, and have access to any medical or therapeutic services that someone wants. Suicide prevention goes beyond keeping people from literally killing themselves, also giving people what they need to live and thrive.

Suicide is the leading cause of death in jail, so abolition itself is suicide prevention.[7] Prison and jail are created to deteriorate mental health, and corrections officers often make this worse. I still remember when I took Introduction to Criminal Justice years ago in college, and it included a tour of the local jail. The corrections officer giving the tour talked about needing to frequently cut people down who tried to hang themselves (the most common method of suicide in jail). I remember him tossing off a "joke" about sometimes taking his time to respond to these calls.

If this seems unbelievable or too extreme, then you probably have not been around many corrections officers, people whose job requires and reinforces dehumanization. But you also don't need to take my word for it. Alisa Roth had a similar experience while researching for *Insane: America's Criminal Treatment of Mental Illness*: "A retired officer told me his colleagues regularly handed razor blades to suicidal prisoners, suggesting the most effective ways for them to slit their wrists."[8]

Our current system not only puts people in situations that create and exacerbate suicidality, it dehumanizes (overwhelmingly) multiply marginalized disabled people to such a point that their lives are seen as having no value at all.

The Problem with the Suicide Hotline

The central suicide resource in the US is what is now called the Suicide and Crisis Lifeline. Whenever someone is struggling with suicidality, the main (and usually only) resource or advice given is to call or text the lifeline. It's become so widely relied on that recently the government made it easier to access by allowing callers and texters to connect by dialing just three numbers: 988.[9] While this may sound like a positive development, one thing I hope you take away from this book is that you can't take it as a given that policies do what they claim to do. You need to look closer.

One huge problem with this arrangement, which the lifeline doesn't publicize much, is that it sometimes calls the police on people. I worked at my local branch of the suicide hotline for a short time about six years ago, when it was called the National Suicide Prevention Lifeline. We were instructed that if we thought someone was in imminent danger of killing themselves then we should try to get their address or use their cell phone information to call their local police and send them to the person.

In 2020, Rob Wipond interviewed me about my experience while writing about the lifeline and their policies on confidentiality for *Mad in America*. In the article, Wipond noted that these "rescues" are rare, according to the lifeline.[10] In my opinion, that all depends on your definition of rare. In my experience—which admittedly was a while ago—on most shifts I would see at least one person call the police. Wipond notes that there are stories all over social media of police showing up at people's houses after they called the lifeline:

> J., a PhD science student and transgender man of
> Middle Eastern heritage, knew about call-tracing but

thought he was safe because he'd bought a disposable phone and, after his call to the Lifeline, removed the battery. Police found him anyway.

His voice shakes as he describes questioning the need for drugs, and a group of men at the hospital grabbing his 5 foot 8, 105-pound frame and holding him down for an injection. "I'm just crying ... Please don't touch me. Please don't touch my body ... One is pressing upon my forehead so hard that I think my glasses are going to break ..."

J. was discharged a week later. "I was so trauma-tized that I dropped out of university," he says, likening the experience to being raped. J. has been working on formal written complaints, but to get past the shame and humiliation, he says, "I have to pretend it wasn't me, that it happened to someone else."[11]

During training at the hotline, I brought up the fact that the police do not respond equally to different people and was immediately dismissed. I cannot speak to now, but at least at that time the well-known biases of the police against both people of color and disabled people were not discussed. Neither was the fact that people involved in the criminal justice system are much more likely to kill themselves.[12] Calling the police on suicidal people just puts those people in situations that are proven to increase the likelihood of suicide.

A suicide hotline is a good idea theoretically, especially because suicide is often impulsive and a big part of acute prevention is distracting someone until the most destruc-tive feelings pass. However, we can't rely on these carceral options run by people who think they know better and are not accountable to the communities they are "serving." Oftentimes, leadership refuses to engage in these conversations and just publicly minimizes their use of the police instead of talking to those of us concerned about why we think it is such a bad idea. (Some suicide lines don't call the police, such as the trans lifeline.) I'm not saying you should never use these services if you are comfortable with the risk, but people should be fully informed about all consequences to their actions, whether they are in crisis or not.

Mandated Treatment

Another way that disabled people are targeted by carceral systems is that they can be incarcerated without even being charged with a crime. Though the specifics of each state's laws differ slightly, every US state has some kind of "mandated treatment" law.[13] A common form of mandated inpatient treatment is colloquially known as a "5150," after the section of the California Welfare and Institutions law that allows psychiatric hospitals to hold people with certain disabilities involuntarily up to seventy-two hours without a hearing if they are deemed a "danger to themselves or others."[14] Under the California law, "grave disability" alone is justification to hold someone. The seventy-two-hour hold can be extended an additional fourteen days if certified by the facility.[15] Though patients are entitled to a hearing, it is an "informal" one, and they are represented by a "patient advocate," not a lawyer. I focused on California because 5150 is so well known, but other states have similar laws. (In the next chapter, I talk about civil commitment, which essentially permits these holds indefinitely.)

Because these laws explicitly focus on people with mental health disabilities, certain diagnoses mean that someone is perpetually at risk of losing their freedom. While these laws are theoretically to help disabled people, they just lead to more harm. One problem is that the places where people are held are not healing and often lead to more issues long-term. Being held somewhere against your will is inherently traumatic.

The purpose of these laws is not to protect or heal disabled people, but to give the state a way to incarcerate them. As noted earlier, incarceration doesn't make anyone safer. This also gives doctors and other medical professionals a pseudo-state power, since they are the ones doing the diagnosing, making the decisions as to whether someone should be held, and writing the reports that the courts use to make their decisions.

Another problem with these laws is that while you are being held, you don't get much say in the medications you are given and can be medicated against your will. In *We've Been Too Patient: Voices from Radical Mental Health*, Jeffrey Goines writes about being forcibly restrained and medicated in the hospital:

> It was a horrifying situation—I was surrounded, restrained, and bracing myself for the inevitable. I didn't hear the order, but I knew what was coming. They stuck me with a hypodermic needle attached to a syringe filled with Haldol. Haldol is a miserable first-generation neuroleptic (a.k.a. antipsychotic), whose short-term side effects include hallucinations, sedation, drooling, compulsive pacing, diarrhea, and muscle aches. I had pleaded with the doctor and nurses to take the medication orally, since that would have cushioned the anvil-like impact of the drug on my mind and body. I knew about the federal statute mandating that patients who are willing to take medication orally can't be forcibly injected, but the law didn't protect me that night. I was left on a stretcher writhing in restraints as the delusional psychosis of the antipsychotic set in.[16]

Forty-seven states also have so-called "assisted outpatient treatment" laws that allow forcible medication of disabled people even in the absence of incarceration. However, studies have found that these laws don't improve outcomes and are based on false assumptions.[17]

No one should be forced into treatment. Just because someone is disabled does not mean that they should not have the same right to self-determination and bodily autonomy that nondisabled people have.

Peer Services

Along with getting rid of coercive policies, we also need to develop noncarceral ways to support each other. One option is to create and invest in true peer services. I hesitate to even use the word *peer* in this context because it has become so "professionalized" (which I talk more about in the chapter on social work), but when I say "peer" I mean that no one necessarily has more formal education than another person. If one person is getting paid to be there and one person is not, they are not peers.

In the landmark 1977 book *On Our Own: Patient-Controlled Alternatives to the Mental Health System*, Judi Chamberlin explains the importance of "patient-led" alternatives:

> Patient-controlled alternatives can provide services to people without the demoralizing consequences of the authoritarian, hierarchical structure of traditional mental health services. When the emphasis is on people helping one another, the gulf between "patient" and "staff" disappears. Someone can seek help from others without being thought of as sick or helpless. The same person who seeks help can also offer it.[18]

Care facilities are almost always hierarchical, with the providers having much more power than the patients. Some may argue that this is necessary because the health professionals have expertise that patients don't. However, this ignores the knowledge that comes from living in a disabled body. It sets up a disempowering dynamic in which patients are not listened to because only the nurses and doctors are seen as having worthwhile knowledge.

Chamberlin helped to create the Mental Patients Association (MPA). The MPA was a group of ex-patients who came together to run an organization that later opened residences as well. Chamberlin explained the framework of the residence: "Decision making is in the hands of the residents. This includes not only trivial day-to-day decisions—what should be served for dinner, for example—but also major ones. Prospective new residents are accepted into the house by the vote of current residents."[19]

Chamberlin stresses the importance of real decision-making power and calls out organizations that allow participants to make only surface decisions, like what movie to watch, or allow participants to "interview" applicants but give them no actual decision-making power. The noncoercive aspect of the services is an important part of them, as is the disabled-led approach. This is a great example of one of the tenets of disability justice: leadership by the most impacted. Unfortunately, after a lot of great work, the MPA closed due to financial issues.

It's important to note that it doesn't matter what resources are possible if an organization can't remain open. People talk about defunding the police and putting that money into services, and I agree, with the caveat that we need to look very closely at these services and consider them using the principles of abolition, disability justice, and the other liberatory theories we have available.

Caretaking is hard, but we are all already doing it every day in big and small ways for each other, disabled and not. It is also a skill, and you do need to have certain knowledge to do a good job, but this information can be taught to be people who may not be able to jump through the artificial hoops of the education system.

I would go a step further and say that the opportunity to take care of someone can be a reward in itself. While caretaking is incredibly stressful, it can also be very rewarding and generative for people. No one is obligated to give more than they can, just as we are able.

Informal Community Support
Much of this book is made up of suggestions for policy change, but I also wanted to give some concrete suggestions we can

implement ourselves. Many of the people in my life (including myself) have intense struggles with mental health and fear that the only way to get the care we need is to go into the hospital, which always involves at least some trauma.

One of the things I do to help friends in mental health crises who are trying to stay out of the hospital (and they do to help me) is to help them figure out what they need that the hospital has and to see if we can create that in a noncarceral setting where they are in control. If it's the monitoring they need, then we can set up a plan for that. If it's a change of medication, we can help them get and attend an appointment. If it's someone to be available to talk to, we can do that. If it's a rest (which is common under capitalism!), then maybe we can crowdfund a short vacation. I'm not saying that people should never go to the hospital, especially if that is what they think is best and they are making that decision on their own.

In one of the essays in *We've Been Too Patient*, Kelechi Ubozoh discusses being supported in a similar way:

> When I was so depressed I couldn't get out of bed, my friends brought me groceries. My friends took me to poetry readings and hiking in the redwoods, brought me to dance classes and karaoke, invited me to dinner, and sent me inspirational texts featuring unicorns and/or vampires. One friend made sure we had a weekly walking date to check in on me and give me some physical activity. A friend in New York sent me an adult coloring book and crayons. Another friend brought me to an art exhibit called The Black Woman Is God, where I got to see beautiful creations from Black women all over the world. Some friends called, other friends sent emails....
>
> None of these acts of kindness required a background in therapy—just plain old thoughtfulness and care, which any human is capable of doing. Nothing was too small to make a difference. What I needed was

connection and an interruption to the isolation and negative thoughts in my head.[20]

Of course, this does require having a community of people who are able and willing to assist you in these ways, which a lot of us don't have. My disabilities make me feel so isolated, and I don't necessarily have people I can count on to do these things for me. It's okay if you don't either. This is just one of the infinite tools we have or can create.

Access to Appropriate Therapy

Yes, I spent a lot of this section critiquing the professionalized therapeutic model, but that doesn't mean that therapy provided by professionals can't be helpful.

Everyone should have access to culturally appropriate therapists educated in our modalities of choice. We should also have access to therapists who look like us and have had life experiences similar to ours. I like therapy and get a ton out of it. Other people choose not to use it or will engage at certain times and not others. Similar to medical care, just because it is based on the medical model doesn't mean we shouldn't engage with it when it can be helpful (as we define it) for us. Further, people need to be able to talk openly about suicide without fear of being locked up.

Conclusion

This chapter barely scratches the surface of just a few of the concepts we can use to help us think about being able to take care of each other. Police and prisons soak up so many resources that it's hard to even imagine how different the world could look if those resources were devoted to keeping us all actually safe, instead of creating the illusion of security for some at the expense of the safety of others. We always need to remember that we don't need to settle for the systems that currently exist. We can make our own.

Foundational Sources

Ben-Moshe, Liat, Chris Chapman, and Allison C. Carey, eds. *Disability Incarcerated: Imprisonment and Disability in the United States and Canada.* New York: Palgrave Macmillan, 2014.

Chamberlin, Judi. *On Our Own: Patient-Controlled Alternatives to the Mental Health System.* Lawrence, MA: National Empowerment Center, 1997.

Green, L.D., and Kelechi Ubozoh, eds. *We've Been Too Patient: Voices from Radical Mental Health.* Berkeley, CA: North Atlantic Books, 2019.

Metzl, Jonathan M. *The Protest Psychosis: How Schizophrenia Became a Black Disease.* Boston: Beacon Press, 2009.

Roth, Alisa. *Insane: America's Criminal Treatment of Mental Illness.* New York: Basic Books, 2018.

Shimrat, Irit. *Call Me Crazy: Stories from the Mad Movement.* Vancouver: Press Gang Books, 1997.

Long-Term Care

Commentators often say that "correctional facilities are the nation's largest mental health providers," but rarely do they think further about what that actually means. I do want to note that I don't love the way this phrase frames prisons as "treatment," because as you'll see below, even treatment isn't treatment. I don't think considering prison and jail as "treatment" of any kind is accurate or helpful. However, the fact that this is such a common way to describe the relationship between mental health disabilities and US prisons means that people with mental health disabilities are being locked up in prisons disproportionately. This may seem obvious, but my point is that we all know that something is wrong with the way our carceral systems deal with mental health disabilities, but we don't look further into how or why or what to do about it. This chapter gives some insights and ideas.

It's not just mental health disabilities that are overrepresented in prison populations, but physical ones as well. However, researchers tend to focus solely on mental health disabilities, so some of these sections only talk about that. Typically, these categories are not even very well defined and it's not clear how people are categorized. For example, it's not clear whether people with intellectual disabilities are included or what diagnostic tools were used. Even with the best health care, mental health and other disabilities can be hard for doctors to diagnose, and prisons have terrible health care. This also creates a false division between physical and mental health and disabilities, yet they often travel together. I think people also assume that people with physical disabilities who are in facilities need to be there, but that's not true, as I discuss later in this chapter.

It's impossible to know exactly what proportion of incarcerated people are disabled, and study results differ, likely due to methodology. The lowest estimates are around one-third, but most recent studies find that the majority (more than 50 percent) of people in prison are disabled.[1] Though the numbers may differ a bit, no one disagrees that disabled people are overrepresented in prisons. As I've noted throughout this book, disabled people of color are the most affected by these disparities. A recent study used 2016 data to find that 42 percent of the prison population (state and federal) are disabled people of color—42 percent![2]

We know that prisons and jails are full of disabled people. However, there is also a shadow system that exists that includes other places where disabled people are locked up or have other fundamental autonomy taken from them. These places usually exist under a rationale of "caring" for disabled people, though some exist explicitly for other reasons, such as "community safety" or "public health." These policies extend incarceration beyond just prisons and jails, and the state has the power to lock up people who haven't even committed a "crime."

An "institution," as it is usually used in this context, refers to a wide variety of places, such as hospitals, nursing homes, halfway and transitional housing, and other places of congregate living. The material conditions of these places vary tremendously. Some may provide some kind of useful medical treatment—many don't—but often the traumatic effects outdo any kind of healing that may take place.

What these places have in common is that disabled people are forced there against their will through state action. This includes through direct control, like judge-mandated inpatient treatment, and through less obvious ways, like health care benefit policy that only covers inpatient treatment. In all these cases, being disabled alone is enough to lose basic autonomy.

Healing versus Care

First, I want to make a distinction between healing and care. In the institutional context, "care" usually means "in custody of," like when someone is "in the care" of an institution. Healing, however, means a person is actually feeling better—as that person defines it. This is important, because lots of nondisabled people think that there is healing that happens in these places, and for the most part that just isn't true. Even if there are some aspects of healing, they are almost always outweighed by the vast harms there.

Our goal needs to be healing, and not just care. To once again use the map analogy, we need to first figure out where we want to eventually get to. Remember, we are not limited to the options that currently exist and we should not feel constricted by them, especially during the planning stages. We need to be free to dream beyond what we are taught is possible. Not in a utopian sense, but in the very pragmatic sense that limiting our imagination is a strategy by the state to keep us complicit. Therefore, we need to think about what noncarceral healing could look like and build that instead of being limited to just tweaking the current systems.

The Line between Prisons and Institutions Is Not Clear

Throughout this chapter, I'm writing as if there is a clear line between prisons and (what I'm calling generally) "institutions," but there isn't. More and more mental health services are acting carceral, and more jails and prisons are claiming to provide "treatment."

It's important to also talk about the differences between institutions and prisons. Though both are places of incarceration—and there are many opportunities for solidarity to be built between movements—the living conditions can be different. Part of "both/and" is talking about the similarities *and* differences between all of these things. Our activism should be different for different situations, and we can't fine-tune it without understanding the nuances.

All this said, I am not going to compare and contrast prisons and other institutions in this book, but I want to make absolutely clear that while there is overlap, there are also important differences. Even from institution to institution and prison to prison there can be big differences in autonomy and access to basic needs like decent food and rest. The more access you have to money, whiteness, and insurance, the more freedom and small dignities you will likely be afforded in any hospital or institution.

Needy versus Dangerous

A recurring theme throughout disability and criminal justice history is an attempt to split disabled people into one of two groups: needy and dangerous. "Needy" people are funneled to institutions, and "dangerous" people to prison and jail. While both of these categories lead to incarceration, they differ in important ways.

Whether a disabled person is categorized as needy or as dangerous depends largely on their other identities. This is illustrated by both the history of incarceration and current demographics of who is locked up. The difference between who is needy and who is dangerous isn't about someone's likelihood to commit crime, but someone's relationship to power.

To be considered needy, you not only need to be disabled, you also have to be white. I don't want to make it sound like being considered needy is a prize; as we see by how people are treated in institutions, it's also an inhumane categorization. It can, though, come with material benefits that being considered dangerous does not. I'm not trying to say that prisons are better or worse than institutions, but when people are forced into the (terrible) choice, some do choose jail or prison over institutions. However, being labeled "dangerous" removes even the veneer of benefits, treatment, or care.

Where Institutions Came From

Institutions for people with mental health and intellectual disabilities are one of the most obvious ways the carceral state openly targets disabled people. The full history of institutions is beyond the scope of this book, so I am only going to give a few brief highlights (or lowlights.)

Much of US law is borrowed from English common law, and the Elizabethan Poor Laws in the late 1500s and early 1600s still influence the way we look at poverty and disability.[3] Before these laws, the government had no responsibility to materially help people in need. These laws also gave the government the power to imprison people just for being poor.

Poor Law divided people who need assistance into three categories: "vagrant," "involuntary unemployed," and "helpless." People classified as vagrants, or "able-bodied unemployed," could be arrested.[4] Some disabled people—along with widows and orphans and the "frail elderly"—were considered "worthy" poor and could get some help from the government. It created a system where the state decides who "deserves" help and who "deserves" jail. This created the split between "worthy" poor and "unworthy" poor.

Even though theoretically disabled people are considered "worthy," the understanding of disability that we had centuries ago meant that only certain kinds of disabled people were recognized as "helpless." This structure sets up an oppositional framework between the state and the individual in which it's in the state's interest to define these categories as narrowly as possible.

Until the mid-1800s, the "poorhouse" was the catchall place for disabled people who could not work and weren't able to be supported by their family.[5] The conditions in these poorhouses were terrible, because the government wanted it to be as painful as possible to be poor. They saw poverty as a moral failing, not a failure of capitalism. The bad conditions were supposed to be motivational and are built into this system.

Because disability and poverty are so related, laws helping poor people will affect disabled people, and vice versa.

During the nineteenth century, reformers like Dorothea Dix saw the terrible conditions in jails and poorhouses and noticed that many of the people there had mental health disabilities.[6] Dix and others advocated for special institutions for the mentally ill, in large part to get them away from the "criminals" and other people considered dangerous in jails, prisons, and poorhouses or almshouses.

While this was no doubt well intentioned, it furthered the divide between worthy and unworthy and reinforced that some people deserve help and others don't. This was racialized as well, and many of the places created for disabled people barred people of color. By virtue of their skin color, many disabled people are considered inherently unworthy.

Conditions in Institutions

There are many accounts that detail the terrible conditions and the horrors that happened—and continue to happen—in institutions for disabled people. They were uniformly disgusting and neglectful and led to the torture and premature death of many disabled people. It's not controversial to say these places were horrible and inhumane. As with everything else, conditions varied, and those people with the most resources and who needed the least support tended to have the best outcomes.

And as usual in the US, this was extremely racialized. If conditions were bad for white people, they were always worse for Black people and other people of color. In an article titled "An Early History—African American Mental Health," Vanessa Jackson explains:

> African-Americans were frequently housed in public (as opposed to private) facilities such as the poorhouse, jail or the insane asylum. These facilities almost always had

substandard conditions. If conditions in the facility were poor for white patients, conditions were completely inhumane for African-American patients.[7]

Institutions were never meant to help disabled people, especially Black and other multiply marginalized disabled people. Since multiply marginalized disabled people were de facto considered "dangerous," even the places purported to "care" for them were built with a similar carceral intent to prisons and jails. Even the private facilities that catered to white disabled people with resources were created for the benefit of the families of disabled people and not the disabled people themselves, as the conditions make clear.

Institutions developed because (white) disabled people were seen as too worthy to be in the same place as "criminals" (largely nonwhite disabled people). Reformers thought they were helping (white) disabled people. I note this not to give these reformers a pass, but to point out that even when you have good intentions you can end up causing a lot of harm. That's why it's so important that movements are led by the people most affected.

This split into "jails" and "institutions" also coincided with the rise of eugenics (which I discuss in the next chapter), and institutions were another way to keep "defective" women from reproducing. Being court ordered to an institution, and thus under state custody and control, made it that much easier for doctors to later carry out their forced sterilization campaign against disabled women.

Deinstitutionalization

During the second half of the twentieth century, the US started to move away from the institutional model. Deinstitutionalization was a movement made up of disabled people, family members, and other activists who worked to close down institutions. While the movement had relative success and many of these places did close down, deinstitutionalization—especially as actually enacted—was no panacea.

One problem was that the state was more easily convinced to close down these facilities—and thus not to have to pay for them—than it was to create truly community-based care. Many of the places that were created during this period as alternatives to institutions replicated the same issues that the institutions did.

Deinstitutionalization reminds us that abolition requires both building and dismantling. We can learn a lot about strategy from looking at the activism surrounding deinstitutionalization's successes and failures. Not to lionize or demonize people from the past, but to learn how to get even better at both building and tearing down. That said, deinstitutionalization activists deserve way more (metaphorical) flowers than they have been given.

Deinstitutionalization is abolitionist and fits squarely in a disability justice framework. Disabled deinstitutionalization activists made arguments in the 1970s that sound like—and influenced—the more recent disability justice movement. Deinstitutionalization isn't just an event that happened in the past, it is also a theoretical orientation that sees disabled people as full humans who deserve autonomy.

The Myth of Transincarceration

Liat Ben-Moshe's *Decarcerating Disability* looks at the deinstitutionalization movement through an abolitionist lens and was an invaluable resource for this section. In the book, Ben-Moshe describes the concept of "transincarceration" and explodes the myth that deinstitutionalization is responsible for the increase in the prison population.

Transincarceration means going from one site of incarceration to another. For example, many people with mental health disabilities are shuffled between jails and psych wards. The concept of transincarceration acknowledges that prisons and jails aren't the only places where people are incarcerated, and it also notes the frequency of people moving between carceral systems rather than out of them.

Ben-Moshe argues:

> Connecting deinstitutionalization to, not to mention blaming it on, the rise of the U.S. prison nation also leads one to believe that psych hospitals closed and led the same people to be incarcerated in prisons. But this claim cannot be corroborated in terms of demographics.... Over the years, the gender distribution of those in mental hospitals tended to be either equal or trending toward overrepresentation of women. However, in terms of imprisonment, the majority of those newly imprisoned are male. There are differences in terms of age and race as well.[8]

It's a myth that closing institutions led directly to those same people being imprisoned, as the demographics prove. Institutions had a lot of white women, while prisons contain disproportionately Black men. In other words, white people get "care" and nonwhite people get punishment.

This is also obviously a generalization, as there are lots of white people in prisons and people of color in institutions, and both are carceral sites for disabled people. But these differences aren't a coincidence, and they are caused both directly and indirectly by many of the policies I discuss in this book.

In *Reducing Mass Incarceration: Lessons from the Deinstitutionalization of Mental Hospitals in the 1960s*, Bernard Harcourt explains:

> Deinstitutionalization in the 1960s and 1970s drew heavily on predictions of dangerousness. The trouble is that the use of risk assessment tools typically has the effect of sorting on race and increasing racial disproportion within our "dangerous" populations. This was certainly the case with regard to mental hospitals....

The turn to dangerousness had a distinctly disproportionate effect on African American populations: the
proportion of minorities in mental hospitals increased
significantly during the process of deinstitutionalization.
From 1968 to 1978, for instance, there was a significant
demographic shift among mental hospital admittees.[9]

Harcourt's point is a crucial one: deinstitutionalization
was really just deinstitutionalization for white people.

Rationale Is Important

Another reason deinstitutionalization wasn't the success it
could have been was that the rationale for closing institutions
was never about the well-being of disabled people. It was about
the state saving money. It may seem like a win for an institution to be closed—and it may be—but if it's done for austerity
reasons then there will also not be money for supports that
people with disabilities need to live full lives in the community.

Disabled people are disproportionately harmed by focusing only on closures and not on building up other supports,
since we are more likely to need those services to be able to
perform the basic functions of living. And in the meantime, a
lack of services means many disabled people will end up in
carceral structures.

This is not to say that there may not be times in your
community when pushing the cost savings may be a useful
strategy, but be careful and know that this line of thinking will
likely be harmful for disabled people. We need to be thoughtful
and nuanced and center multiply marginalized disabled people.

Institutions in the Current Day

When we think about institutions, a lot of times we just think
about institutions for people with psychological disabilities,
but people with developmental and intellectual disabilities and
neurodiverse people are still consistently being institutionalized.

Many people think these institutions are a thing of the past, but not only do institutions still exist, some openly use dangerous and painful methods to get disabled people to comply. One facility that does this is the Judge Rotenberg Center (JRC) in Canton, Massachusetts.

The JRC uses an electric shocking device that it created on the neurodiverse people who are forced to live there. Lydia X.Z. Brown hosts an archive of JRC abuses and writes that six people have died while at the institution (formerly known as the Behavior Research Institute). The electric devices were made to be more powerful than a police taser and are used for behavior modification. According to Brown: "In addition to contingent electric shock, BRI/JRC has also used extremely prolonged restraint, food deprivation, deep muscle pinching, forced inhalation of ammonia, and sensory assault techniques for behavior modification."[10]

Even as I write this, the JRC is still using these electric shock torture devices on people. Though the FDA banned the use of these devices in 2020, the DC Circuit Court of Appeals overturned this ban in July 2021. At the time of writing, the JRC continues to use the torture device on some of its residents.[11] It's unconscionable that institutionalized disabled people continue to be tortured like this.

Even if you believe that some kind of congregate setting is appropriate for disabled people (which I don't), what happens openly at these places is still enough for them to be shut down. These are not places of healing and treatment; they are usually useless at best, torturous and deadly at worst. I could go on (and on and on), but the poor conditions and treatment in institutions continues today.

Civil Commitment

The last several decades have seen a huge growth in civil commitment. Civil commitment laws allow the government to imprison people outside of a criminal conviction or sentence.

For example, states have passed laws that allow them to continue to hold people deemed "sexually violent predators" (SVPs) even past the maximum sentence allowed by law for their convictions. Maya Schenwar and Victoria Law describe civil commitment in their book *Prison by Any Other Name: The Harmful Consequences of Popular Reforms*:

> The indefinite involuntary civil commitment specifically created for people convicted of sex offenses is an insidious reform that emerged three decades ago and has since multiplied exponentially. Though they're labeled treatment centers and fall within the civil—not criminal—legal realm, these facilities essentially serve as prisons. They hold people whose prison terms have legally ended who are mandated to undergo continual monitoring and treatment, frequently leading to a lifetime of confinement. These are places where people are confined because of an alleged psychiatric diagnosis (such as pedophilia), not because of a conviction; punishment for the conviction has already been meted out, but confinement-based "treatment" for the diagnosis could be never ending.[12]

This poorly defined label plays on racist and ableist myths about safety and allows the state to incarcerate someone indefinitely at its whim. The "treatment facilities" where people deemed SVPs are usually sent are known for having especially bad conditions.[13]

Civil commitment sits squarely at the intersection of disability and incarceration and deserves more focus from abolitionists. It gives the state power to indefinitely incarcerate people who have not been convicted of crimes or have already served their time. People who are confined under civil commitment laws are usually sent to locked wards of hospitals or the other kinds of institutions I've described in this chapter.

I discussed the problem of addressing sexual violence with carceral responses in an earlier chapter, but that's not nearly the only problem with SVP designation and civil commitment. The issue is much bigger than I have the space for, but it's important to note that these labels could have the practical effect of someone spending the rest of their lives incarcerated without having committed a crime. This "diagnosis" is based in criminal justice, not medicine or any other science, and is not well defined. This gives those doing the labeling carceral power that disproportionately affects disabled and other marginalized people because of stereotypical associations among race, disability, and perceived dangerousness.

The civil commitment statutes rely on diagnoses and labels, which as I discussed earlier are subjective and heavily influenced by racism, colonialism, and ableism. It's even more unjust in these scenarios, because the doctors usually have relationships with the criminal justice system and are subject to influence. Even well-meaning doctors have to rely largely on records and observations created by people employed by the state. Civil commitment is an important issue that people who care about abolition and disability justice need to organize around together.

Nursing Homes and Group Homes

Nursing homes and group homes are other places where disabled people are warehoused. In many ways they are just smaller-scale institutions. No matter how nice and "homey" they may be, the fact is that nursing homes and group homes are not homes, or else they would just be called that. Nursing homes and group homes are congregate care settings that are run by systems and corporations, whether nonprofit or for-profit. Many people end up in this housing because it's the only kind of supportive housing they have access to.

Note that I am not talking about cooperative living situations where residents can share professional care and medical services, but places that require unnecessarily giving up some autonomy for care (which are pretty much all of them).

There are material differences between nursing homes and other kinds of institutions that can make them more livable, and the treatment one gets even between nursing homes varies widely. Moving from an institution to a group home may be a huge positive change for an individual, and I would never fault someone for making the choice (though the disabled person rarely has much choice in the matter). However, on a systemic level, for true deinstitutionalization to happen we also need to abolish nursing homes.

Guardianships

Disabled people don't have to be in a physical institution for the state to be complicit in restricting their rights. Guardianships are legal relationships in which the state gives a "guardian" decision-making ability over another person. This decision-making power may be over every part of someone's life, including their body and medical decisions, or one specific part, like their money. (Conservatorships are guardianships but specifically just over finances.)

The rationale behind guardianships is that due to disability, one person is unable to make their own decisions and someone else needs to make those decisions for them. This is different from a power of attorney, in which someone can do business on your behalf or make medical decisions if you are incapacitated but you also have the power to make your own decisions. Guardianships essentially create a legal relationship similar to that between a parent and a minor child.

This happens all the time to disabled people, and every time a guardianship is approved rights are necessarily taken away. Sometimes a disabled person will lose the choice to remain at home, which is common with elder disabled people. (While age often disables, it doesn't always, especially if one has the resources to maintain their health as much as possible.)

One of the most famous examples of a guardianship is Britney Spears. Spears's dad, Jamie, acted as the singer's conservator from 2008 to 2021, after a public struggle with mental health issues.[14] Though the conservatorship theoretically just gave Jamie control over Britney's finances, the elder Spears was able to leverage this power to take over every aspect of Britney's life. This included matters as personal as reproductive decisions, and Britney testified that Jamie would not let the singer take out an IUD that had been implanted.[15]

If this can happen to a rich and famous person, it can—and does—happen to less powerful disabled people all the time. Though most disabled people aren't as profitable for their guardians as Spears, many get benefits that guardians may have access to. Further, many health care (and other) companies make fortunes off of disabled people, including through the guardianship and conservatorship fees a disabled person can be required to pay even when the guardianship is against their will.

The Problem with Least Restrictive Environment

One of the most famous disability rights cases is *Olmstead v. L.C.*[16] This Supreme Court case from 1999 dealt with the rights of disabled people to live in the community instead of institutions. Two disabled women sued the state of Georgia to be provided with community supports outside of the institution so they could leave. The court in *Olmstead* held that disabled people have a right to treatment in the community instead of institutions *if* certain conditions are met. Those conditions are that treatment professionals think that community supports are appropriate, the person does not object to living in the community, and the community services would be a reasonable accommodation considering what similarly disabled people frequently need. *Olmstead* means that only *some* disabled people have the right to live in the "least restrictive environment" (LRE).

In other words, disabled people's right to live in the community is qualified, not guaranteed. Late disability activist and professor Steve Taylor (who coincidentally is the person who helped me to get the accommodations I needed to finish law school) explained that "the question imposed by LRE is not whether the rights of people with developmental disabilities should be restricted, but to what extent."[17] Many organizations that purport to serve people with mental illness don't push for deinstitutionalization, but instead push for "options." As long as one of the options is an institution, disabled people will be locked up there against our will, especially as we are often perceived as lacking decision-making capability.

The Problem with "Community Mental Health"

Many abolitionists talk about "community mental health" without thinking about what that means. Just because something is physically outside of an institution doesn't necessarily make it abolitionist. Community mental health can mean so many different things, and abolitionists need to be very specific when we are talking about the kinds of mental health resources we want to create. Community mental health doesn't necessarily mean noncarceral.

It's important to look critically at "community mental health treatment" to determine if something really is community based or not. This boils down to the actual power that residents have over their spaces and lives. Anything less than what nondisabled people have is unacceptable.

Moving toward Healing

There is sometimes a false binary in long-term care, in that the choice is seen as between the state providing all of the "care" or the family doing all of it. One of the big questions that people have about abolition of carceral long-term care is, "What will we do with disabled people?" The tone of the question varies by speaker and likelihood of incarceration. This chapter gives just a few of the infinite answers to providing long-term care for everyone, but especially people who currently rely on the state for some of their care needs.

With the right resources, almost everyone could live in the community right now, whether by themselves, with friends or family, or in another arrangement. Some people will of course need more resources than others, and some of these may or may not be available at this moment, but full inclusion is what we should aim for.

I'm not saying that we currently have the resources and technology for every single disabled person to live in the setting they want, but we can start working toward that. What doesn't exist yet can be built. However, it can't be created until we dream of it first.

What Do We Want to Create?

I don't have the space to fully examine all of the "alternatives" to carceral long-term care that have existed and currently exist, nor do I agree with the framing of "alternatives" in the first place, since it positions care in relation to carceral systems. This leaves behind the "ideological footprint" that Mariame Kaba talks about.[18] Even if we are just using it as a guide of what *not* to do and where *not* to go, it's still part of the building plans.

Instead, we need to start by dreaming about what would be best for us and then work to get there. In my map analogy, this is California. It's what I mean when I talk about figuring out our destination so we know where we are going. What actually helps healing? That's what we should build. Of course, it's not necessarily possible to get there overnight, but I'm not claiming that it is. People assume that abolitionist reforms have to be things that would be considered "radical" by the mainstream, but that's not always the case. (I personally wouldn't care if it was, but the fact is that it's not.) For example, one popular and often abolitionist reform is increasing access to in-home care.

Forcing someone to go to a hospital or other institution for care that could be given at home necessarily requires them giving up freedoms just by nature of being there and not having the freedom to live at home. Of course, not all care can currently be done safely in someone's home, and I'm not saying that some level of home care is the solution for everyone who needs long-term care. The whole point is that different people need different things, and we are not limited to only one solution or kind of care. There are so many things we can do, including those that have yet to be dreamed of, and home care is just one of many resources that we should all have access to that can help people have less interaction with carceral systems.

As I've explained throughout this book, the current systems came out of the "reforms" of past ones. The aim was to do something different than what existed, but since there wasn't a larger vision, many of the reforms that are sold as decreasing the impact of the criminal justice system and increasing safety are proven to do the opposite. All reformist reforms pay attention to is whether we are moving from where we are starting, but they don't distinguish whether those changes bring us closer to the world we want or not. This wouldn't be a problem if everything was as it seemed on its face, but we currently live in a world where people make money based on incarceration, both directly through investments and indirectly from using fear of the carceral state to preserve capitalist "order."

Therefore, under our current system, it is in the interests of those with power to increase both the size and strength of the carceral system. One way they do this is by justifying and selling some of these policies as humane "reforms" instead of what they are, which is new markets in which to make money. We need a system of care designed around the needs of disabled people, not the markets. As we can see throughout this book, reformist reforms strengthen the carceral state, and only abolition can lead to liberation.

We Don't Need Institutions

To once again quote Ben-Moshe:

> One of the most pervasive arguments against deinsti-
> tutionalization ... is the widespread belief that certain
> people will always require some custodial care. This is
> especially the case for people with cognitive, psychiatric,
> and intellectual/developmental disabilities—especially
> for those whose labels are on the "severe or profound"
> side of the spectrum. Many professionals, and parents,
> believe that the best interests of "these people" will
> always be better served in residential settings, and
> although others can benefit from programs and ther-
> apies, they cannot....
>
> Such discourses reproduce tropes of some disa-
> bled people as innocent and eternal children. Under
> the discourse of innocence, social, political, and legal
> recognition is only inferred on those who are deemed
> as normative and nonthreatening, which are racialized
> and gendered constructs.[19]

The truth is that no one needs to be in an institution. There
are other ways to provide literally everything anyone—including disabled people—would need. And anything that doesn't
currently exist can be created.

Beyond "Police, Prisons, and Institutions"

Abolitionists trying to include a disability justice perspective in
their work will tack on institutions to the list of things we need
to abolish: police, prisons, and institutions. They're not wrong,
as closing institutions is important and the deinstitutionalization movement is something that abolitionists can learn from.
However, the relationship between disability justice and abolition goes far beyond just closing institutions.

The following chapters explore the ways that US systems
and policies that encourage criminal justice involvement target

disabled people and make it more likely we will be incarcerated or have other fundamental autonomy taken from us. The differing rationales behind prisons, jails, institutions, and other carceral locales require different approaches to abolition.

Foundational Sources

Ben-Moshe, Liat. *Decarcerating Disability: Deinstitutionalization and Prison Abolition*. Minneapolis: University of Minnesota Press, 2020.

Schenwar, Maya, and Victoria Law. *Prison by Any Other Name: The Harmful Consequences of Popular Reforms*. New York: The New Press, 2020.

The Medical System

Health care—and lack of—is a subtext that runs through so many aspects of incarceration, yet it is rarely directly addressed. Access to health care contributes both directly and indirectly to the growth of prisons and other carceral systems and increases the chances that someone will end up incarcerated.

Lack of Health Care = Incarceration

The structure of the health care system has a huge effect on society, especially carceral systems. Because you need health insurance to access health care, not having health insurance (and therefore no health care) is related to a higher risk of incarceration.[1] The relationship is so strong that after the Affordable Care Act (ACA, aka "Obamacare") expanded health insurance eligibility to more people, arrests went down.[2]

We know that there are a lot of people with mental health and other disabilities in jails and prisons, and part of the reason they are there is because there is not any meaningful accessible treatment. If there is, it usually requires giving up rights and being subject to further surveillance that may lead to increased contact with the criminal justice system.

Further, while people are incarcerated there is no meaningful access to health care. Though jails and prisons are constitutionally required to provide health care for the people incarcerated there, and theoretically every facility has medical staff and an infirmary (or something similar), in practice there is no or very little helpful medical care in jails and prisons. That means that once someone is incarcerated, they are

essentially deprived of health care. For disabled people especially—who are more likely to rely on medications or other
substances—this lack of care can lead to withdrawals or an
increase of symptoms that in turn can lead to further disability
and even death. I discuss this in more detail in the chapter on
disablement.

How We Got Here

To understand the way the medical system interacts with
disabled bodies today, we need to discuss how it came about.
As I've said many times, it was never created to help disabled
people live fulfilling lives. In fact, a lot of the medical system
as we know it was built for the purpose of eliminating disabled people altogether, through a long history of eugenics that
continues today.

Eugenics

Fuck baseball, it's actually eugenics that is America's greatest
pastime. Eugenics is the limitation of reproductive freedom
for members of society deemed "less desirable" and the policies that encourage reproduction in those favored by society
(read: white and nondisabled). Dorothy Roberts wrote about
eugenics in the groundbreaking book *Killing the Black Body:
Race, Reproduction, and the Meaning of Liberty*:

> By 1913 twenty-four states and the District of Columbia
> had enacted laws forbidding marriage by people
> considered genetically defective, including epileptics,
> imbeciles, paupers, drunkards, criminals, and the
> feebleminded....
>
> The eugenics movement, however, did not rely on
> nature to eliminate the unfit. It implemented a more
> direct means of weeding out undesirable citizens. The
> movement's most lasting legacy is coercive enforcement
> of negative eugenics, which aimed to prevent socially

undesirable people from procreating. Eugenicists advocated compulsory sterilization to improve society by
eliminating its "socially inadequate" members.[3]

As Roberts points out, eugenics wasn't and isn't a fringe
ideology; it was encoded in the laws and approved by the
US Supreme Court. *Buck v. Bell* is a 1927 case that centered
on Carrie Buck, a poor white Virginia woman who was
the test case of a new law that allowed sterilization of the
"feebleminded."[4]

Buck was a live-in domestic worker who was raped and
impregnated by a relative of the homeowners.[5] After the pregnancy, the matron of the house sent Buck away to the State
Colony for Epileptics and Feeble Minded in Virginia, where
Buck's mother had also spent some time. Unfortunately for
Buck, the superintendent at the institution was a major propo-
nent of eugenics named Dr. Priddy.

After successful lobbying by Dr. Priddy and other prom-
inent eugenicists, in 1924 Virginia passed a law that allowed
sterilization of those deemed mentally unfit. However, it was
unclear whether this law would pass constitutional muster, so
Dr. Priddy used Buck as a test case. In violation of legal (and
general) ethics, Buck's lawyer was chosen by Dr. Priddy and
did not launch much of a defense. This was an injustice not
just to Buck but also to other similarly situated people. The
law was held to be constitutional after the sham trial. In the
famous opinion, Supreme Court Justice Oliver Wendell Holmes
Jr. proclaimed "three generations of imbeciles are enough."

Throughout all this, there was never any proof that Buck
was "feebleminded." School records show average grades
before she left school at twelve to work, as was common for
poor rural girls of the time. I include this detail not to argue
that it's somehow more unjust because Buck wasn't disabled—
it wouldn't be any better or worse if she weren't—but to note
how the categories of disability and deviance and poverty

interact with and inform each other. In a detail that makes my stomach hurt, the child born before the sterilization was adopted by Buck's former employers—the ones who had her institutionalized—before dying in childhood.

While the Virginia sterilization law itself was repealed in 1974, *Buck v. Bell* remains good law and has been used by courts even as late as 2001, when an Eighth Circuit appeals court wrote:

> It is true that involuntary sterilization is not always unconstitutional if it is a narrowly tailored means to achieve a compelling government interest. It is also true that the mentally handicapped, depending on their circumstances, may be subjected to various degrees of government intrusion that would be unjustified if directed at other segments of society.[6]

Though in this case the court denied immunity to a social service worker accused of coercing a disabled person into a tubal ligation, it made chillingly clear that nonconsensual sterilization of disabled people is legally allowed under some circumstances.

Eugenics and Race

It wasn't just disability that eugenicists focused on, it was also race. Disabled people of color were at special risk of being sterilized without their knowledge or against their will.

Black people in the South were given nonconsensual sterilizations so frequently that it was called a "Mississippi appendectomy"—"appendectomy" because of how common the procedure was, and also because that was the lie the doctors would tell to women to get them to "consent" to the surgery. From Roberts's book *Fatal Invention*:

> Eugenicists easily latched on to race as an integral element of their ideology. Moreover, the chattel slavery

and Jim Crow systems that violently enforced racial classifications paved the way for the dehumanizing programs that implemented eugenicist ideology. Forced sterilizations, eugenicists' favorite remedy for social problems, were an extension of the brutality inflicted on black Americans. Slaveholders' total dominion over the bodies of enslaved Africans—including ownership of enslaved women's wombs, which they exploited for profit—provided an early model of reproductive control.[7]

Puerto Rican women were also especially targeted by eugenic programs after mainland eugenicist Clarence Gamble implemented a whole sterilization program in Puerto Rico in the 1940s. Sterilization there became so common it was colloquially called "*la operación*." In a chapter in *Undivided Rights: Women of Color Organize for Reproductive Justice*, Elena R. Gutiérrez explains how widespread these surgeries were:

> Within a few years tubal ligation was so common that sterilizing Puerto Rican women after childbirth was almost routine, with consent often obtained either during labor or right after childbirth. Legally, women were to be "well-advised" of the medical justifications for sterilization, but in reality they seldom were and many of the women didn't understand that the procedure was irreversible.[8]

Disability is often used as a pretext for race. As mentioned throughout this book, ableism and racism are intertwined in ways that can't be teased out. Because nonwhite people are culturally constructed by the people in power as "defective" white people, anything the state can do to disabled people it will do disproportionately to people of color, especially disabled ones. The definition of "disability" is dynamic, which can be a tool in the right hands but is used as a weapon by the state.

Current-Day Eugenics

While coercive sterilization doesn't happen as much as it used to, it still does happen today. One way it's carried out is through cases in which the court affirms eugenic agendas, like the Eighth Circuit opinion quoted above. However, eugenics also takes other forms. While they are not usually thought of as eugenics, any policies that make it harder for disabled people to reproduce and parent are eugenics. This includes child protective services (which I discuss in a later chapter) and making pregnancy itself a criminalized state.

In *Policing the Womb: Invisible Women and the Criminalization of Motherhood*, Michele Goodwin looks at the ways the state uses the criminal justice system to deprive people—especially Black women—of reproductive autonomy:

> In Tennessee, prosecutors now negotiate plea deals based on women agreeing to sterilization. It is difficult to determine the frequency of such negotiations, particularly in instances where the woman (or man) refuses. Nevertheless, the handful of cases since 2010 in Nashville alone where women have agreed to sterilization as part of their plea deals (and an early release on probation) indicate that such negotiations are occurring.[9]

Goodwin doesn't always mention the disability status of the women, but regardless of how they identify, the court has to deem them "disabled" in order to be able to take their rights away. This may be either because of actual disability or because of the implicit disability created by white supremacy.

Criminalizing Pregnancy

Eugenics is also at play in the way that poor pregnant people are criminalized. Drugs have often been used as a pretext to imprison poor and marginalized pregnant people. One example of these laws is the so-called Cocaine Mom Law, which allows the state to incarcerate pregnant people for using drugs or alcohol. Even setting aside the (important) broader autonomy issues for a moment, these laws aren't successful in improving fetal or maternal health.

The threat of incarceration discourages pregnant people from seeking the care they need. These laws are also counter-productive in terms of getting gestating parents drug treatment, because it disincentivizes being honest about substance use, even if someone has or is trying to quit. Victoria Law shares the story of Alicia Beltran:

> In 2013, Beltran told medical providers that she had taken Suboxone as a way to wean herself off painkillers. When she realized that she was pregnant, she weaned herself off Suboxone. Medical providers insisted that she begin taking Suboxone again; when Beltran refused, she was arrested. Although she was 14 weeks pregnant, police forced her to kneel on the floor before cuffing both her wrists and ankles. She was brought to the jail where she spent an entire day without food or water. Like [others], Beltran was not assigned a lawyer, but her fetus was.
>
> Beltran was ordered into drug treatment for 75 days. During that time, she lost her job. The treatment facility provided no prenatal care, but fortunately Beltran's mother was allowed to drive her from the center to prenatal care two hours away. Had her mother not been willing or able to do so, Beltran would have had to go without; the program did not provide transportation.[10]

Though it may feel like it should be "illegal" for pregnant people to use drugs, in reality such laws are counterproductive. Studies show that poverty has as much, if not more, impact on developing fetuses as maternal crack use does.[11] If we were actually concerned about the well-being of parents and children, we would make sure they had the resources they needed for health.

Doctors as Cops

Another way pregnancy is criminalized is the way doctors are increasingly deputized to carry out "law enforcement" functions. Doctors perform surveillance functions that can have criminal and other penalties that affect liberty and negatively impact the health of patients. Doctors and other medical professionals decide who to test for drugs without the same constitutional restraints that police do in searches. Goodwin explains:

> Cases across the United States illustrate how physicians and hospital staff operate not only as caretakers to their patients, but also interpreters of state statutes. States increasingly seek physicians' appraisal of pregnant women's behavior under the guise of promoting fetal health. Their interventions in women's pregnancies seem far more related to evaluating women's compliance and obedience. Indeed, fetal protection efforts expose legislative antagonism to the interests of low-income pregnant women. Many fetal protection laws are intended to measure women's obedience and not actual fetal risk, since these laws do very little to promote fetal health.[12]

In order to accurately diagnose and treat patients, doctors need to create environments where patients can be honest with them about their behaviors, including illegal ones. These laws exist not to protect children, but to strengthen the prison- and medical-industrial complexes. We know that criminalization is worse for the fetus, but what needs to be more important is the fact that it is worse for the *parent*. In other words, we need to center the person who is pregnant, not the potential person they may birth.

Insurance

The cost of medical care is exorbitant in the US, and no one but the very rich can afford to pay out of pocket. Even in emergency rooms, which are supposed to treat anyone who needs urgent medical care regardless of insurance or ability to pay, people are turned away or discharged without any meaningful care, often with large bills they have no way of paying. The US has made it so that in order to get health care you need insurance, and in order to get insurance you need a job. As I mentioned earlier, since the employment rate of disabled people has been hovering around 20 percent for the last few years, this leaves those who need health care the most as the least able to get it.

However, even having health insurance in the US doesn't guarantee adequate medical care. A common example: many private insurance policies have very high deductibles that require paying a lot out of pocket before you are covered by the insurance, so even though someone is technically insured, they may not have actual access to health care. The kind of insurance you have and what it is willing to cover makes a big difference—literally a life-or-death one—as to whether you can access care.

Even if you have health coverage, insurance companies regularly deny coverage for necessary treatment, which leads to people dying. This is what happened to disability activist Carrie Ann Lucas, who died after her insurance company denied coverage for necessary medication.[13]

Public versus Private Insurance
Like everything about US healthcare, the insurance system is needlessly complicated, and I don't have the space here to talk in more than the broadest strokes. For simplicity's sake, I'm going to divide insurance into public and private.

In the US, there are two kinds of public insurance: Medicare and Medicaid. Generally, in the US, private insurance is obtained through employment of oneself or a family member. One of the many changes of the ACA was that the government created a "marketplace" that lets people buy private health insurance, generally for less than it used to cost. They did this by subsidizing the cost of private insurance. In other words, the government pays private insurance companies on an individual's behalf. Even still, it is still prohibitively expensive for many people—and further, the coverage itself is still often inadequate.

With every policy decision, choices are made. There are many ways that health care could have become more accessible while at the same time not strengthening those that have vested interests in community dis-ease, like the insurance lobby. While the ACA helped some individuals get access to health care, it also further entrenched the private insurance system. There are many problems with this, including keeping health care as a benefit with certain kinds of employment instead of making it a human right. It's especially bad for disabled people when health insurance is tied to employment. Those who are too sick or disabled to work are the least likely to have private health insurance, and thus many have to rely on public insurance, which may not give them the care they actually need.

Public Insurance

Those who cannot afford private insurance may be able to get coverage through public options like Medicaid and Medicare. In order to enroll in these programs, applicants need to meet certain qualifications. For Medicaid there are income limits, and only those who make under a certain amount will qualify. Medicare is provided for people over a certain age, and for disabled people who have qualified for certain kinds of disability benefits. Public insurance is provided by a combination of the federal and state governments (and other funding sources), and the coverage and eligibility varies a lot by state. These are supposed to be similar to private plans, only provided by the government. (Many kinds of public insurance even require recipients to pay for coverage, but I'm setting those aside for now because, as I said, this is an oversimplification.) This setup has in practice created two different segregated medical systems.

This divide is highly racialized, and people of color have much less access to health care than white people. Though the ACA reduced this disparity, it didn't close it. The Kaiser Family Foundation noted the racial disparities between both access to private insurance and insurance in general:

> The higher uninsured rates among [people of color] groups largely reflects more limited rates of private coverage among these groups. While Medicaid and the Children's Health Insurance Program (CHIP) help fill the gap in private coverage for people of color, they do not fully offset the difference, leaving them more likely to be uninsured.[14]

Medical providers can choose which insurances they take, and many don't take public insurance (for reasons also beyond the scope of this chapter, but it boils down to money, of course, and is in large part because public insurance often has lower reimbursement rates). When we are forced to rely on insurance, we are at the mercy of a company whose sole purpose is to make money for shareholders. I talk more about the financial aspect of all this at the end of this chapter, but just on a basic level, the insurance system puts up gates and takes away health resources from the people who need it the most, using the "savings" to line the pockets of the people who need it the least.

Institutional Bias

When insurance companies control access to care, they control how and where you get care. Institutional bias and similar policies are one of the tentpoles holding up the carceral state. Institutional bias in this context occurs when an insurance company is willing to cover care in an institution but is not willing to cover care in the community.

Institutional bias forces people into institutions even when other treatments are better or less expensive, since it's sometimes the only option that insurance will cover. The

Social Security Act requires Medicaid to cover ongoing care needs for disabled people in institutions, but not when they are provided in the disabled person's home.[15] Some states' Medicaid programs will cover home and community-based services, but they don't have to.

So, let's say you get hurt really badly and need help with some of your daily needs. There may be different ways that you can receive this help, like living in a rehabilitation facility or having people come to your house and assist you, such as direct support professionals. Institutional bias means that Medicaid is required to cover these services only in the rehabilitation facility, forcing people into more restricted environments. Policies that carry institutional bias increase the size of and reliance on institutions and take resources away from home- and community-based treatment.

This issue is on the radar of disability justice activists, and several legislative proposals have been introduced to get rid of or reduce institutional bias, though so far none have passed. One notable example was the 2019 Disability Integration Act (DIA), which would have required insurance programs to cover home- and community-based long-term support services as well.[16] Even though the DIA had a bipartisan group of cosponsors and widespread support from influential groups like the AARP, it did not move forward after its initial introduction.

Abolitionists need to pay attention to health care policy, because access to health care is so closely related to incarceration. Poring over insurance legislation isn't necessarily as exciting as literally tearing down walls, but it is how we help keep each other alive to be able to fight another day.

Health Care for Everyone (Obviously!)

Everyone should be able to get the health care they need, which is impossible under the current privatized system. I call the whole system privatized because even though there is insurance provided by the government, medical care itself is almost exclusively provided in the private sector by for-profit and not-for-profit corporations. We need a public system in which everyone is covered. With a public universal system, in the way that I'm using it, there is no "insurance" middleman. If you need to go to the doctor, you go to the doctor, and the doctor is paid by the government.

One notable carve-out to the generally privatized US health care system is the Veterans Affairs (VA) health network in the US. People who qualify for VA health insurance benefits generally are limited to going to VA-run and -funded medical centers. The VA system has a lot of problems, and I am holding it up not as what we should aim for but as an illustration of the difference between public and private systems. (Because it is a microsystem inside of a much larger private system, it doesn't have a lot of the benefits that a public system would have but still carries a lot of the costs.)

In private systems, the motive is profit, which is all siphoned off from people needing care. Think about all the money the current insurance system costs, including corporate salaries and campaign donations, and imagine if that all was redirected into healing. There is also a lot of cost savings in public systems, because people can get preventative care that keeps them from needing more costly interventions. Though empirically proven, the cost savings isn't the point, and in fact the purpose is to move away from valuing cost above lives.

I don't mean that the state as we currently know it should be the only source of care, because that has its own concerns. I mean that we should collectively use resources to provide care to each other. Health care policy is a battleground abolitionists need to be on.

Foundational Sources

Goodwin, Michele. *Policing the Womb: Invisible Women and the Criminalization of Motherhood*. Cambridge: Cambridge University Press, 2020.

Nelson, Alondra. *Body and Soul: The Black Panther Party and the Fight against Medical Discrimination*. Minneapolis: University of Minnesota Press, 2011.

Roberts, Dorothy. *Fatal Invention: How Science, Politics, and Big Business Re-create Race in the Twenty-First Century*. New York: The New Press, 2011.

Roberts, Dorothy. *Killing the Black Body: Race, Reproduction, and the Meaning of Liberty*. New York: Vintage Books, 1997.

Washington, Harriet. *Medical Apartheid: The Dark History of Medical Experimentation on Black Americans from Colonial Times to the Present*. New York: Anchor Books, 2006.

Drugs

You cannot fully understand the connections between disability and incarceration without considering drugs. The National Institute on Drug Abuse estimates that 85 percent of the prison population either have an active substance abuse issue or were incarcerated for a crime related to drugs (including being under the influence at the time of the crime).[1] The intricacies of addiction and drug policy could be a whole series of books, so I'm only going to be painting this issue with the broadest brush. But if there is one thing that you take from this chapter, I hope it is that drug policy is a disability issue. Not all disabled people use drugs, prescribed or otherwise, but drug policy will always have a disproportionate effect on disabled people.

There will always be drugs, and there should be, because drugs can be extremely helpful. And individuals should be able to choose to take or not take them as they want. There will also always be people who use substances in ways they are not comfortable with and want help stopping. I've quit a few substances and it is really difficult. I've used resources like hospital detox centers that helped to make it a little easier, and they could have been much more helpful and less traumatic if I had had actual time with doctors who listened to me. If we focused on making drug treatment available to those who want it and tailoring it to the best outcomes instead of to carceral and capitalist purposes, more people would have access to better healing.

I do not mean to minimize addiction. Addiction is a huge and devastating problem, which is why we need resources that are actually helpful and that don't just expand the criminal justice system. All the resources that are spent on surveillance and forcing people into treatment they don't want should be spent on making noncarceral resources available for people who do want to change their relationships with substances.

The War on Drugs and Disabled People

The War on Drugs is a term that came to prominence during the 1980s, and it refers to a collection of policies and rhetoric that raised penalties for people who use drugs or are involved in the drug trade. These policies increased jail time for drug-related offenses and put more federal resources into surveillance and prosecution of drug crimes, among other things. Essentially, the War on Drugs was a war on people who used drugs, a population that is disproportionately disabled.

The War on Drugs was—and still is—a way to get a lot of disabled people under carceral control. Though some of the rhetoric of the War on Drugs has been abandoned, many of the policies remain, and a lot of disabled people are still incarcerated under them.

I understand that some of the relevant laws and individual practice policies were created to try to protect people from addiction. One recurring theme throughout this book is that "protection" and "care" are rationales that the state frequently uses to incarcerate disabled people. Even by their own terms, these policies are failures.

The carceral approach to drugs has been proven to not work. Jailing and imprisoning people for drug offenses is counterproductive, because it doesn't result in reduced use and actually increases the risk of death. Michele Goodwin notes:

> Incarceration is not linked to a reduction in drug use
> or misuse. Rather, incarceration is associated with
> increased mortality, because within the first two weeks

after incarceration individuals are nearly thirteen times more likely to die—and this is associated with overdose.[2]

Jails and prisons don't provide any meaningful drug treatment. The PEW Charitable Trust reports that of the people who had drug dependencies at the time of arrest, only one person in thirteen received treatment in prison or jail.[3] As you read this chapter, remember that we know what we are doing isn't working, yet we keep doing it. It's important to understand why.

Legal versus Illegal Drugs

When I talk about drugs, I'm referring to both legal and illegal drugs, including alcohol. In part because it's not just "illegal" drugs that are at issue, as even legal drugs require incredible invasions of privacy and can lead to contacts with the criminal justice system in a number of ways.

Also, I think it's both theoretically important to frame the discussion this way and the most accurate, because the line between what's legal and what's not is completely made up and changing all the time. When I first started one of the medications I'm on, it was not a "controlled substance." But the DEA put more restrictions on the medications, and people who rely on them now have to jump through additional hoops, including urine testing. Now I have to pee in a cup, which is then tested for drugs. If it comes up positive for anything I am not supposed to be on, then I am at risk of being discharged from the practice and therefore not able to access the medications I need for my chronic illnesses. While the doctors cannot arrest anyone, taking away access to necessary medications makes incarceration much more likely. Needing certain medications alone increases surveillance.

I eventually ended up going off of this medication, even though it was helpful, because it wasn't worth all the hassle. I want to be clear that no one was worried about addiction in this case, and even my doctors expressed frustration at the new laws, but they felt like they had to follow them whether it was best for their patients or not. Conversely, marijuana—which I also rely on for medication—has become more legal over time.

Whether drugs are illegal is a matter of policy, not morality, though we tend to confuse the two. There is nothing morally wrong with using drugs of any kind, and the line of what is legal and what is illegal is always changing. It also changes state by state, and it isn't necessarily based on safety, as alcohol is more dangerous but more legal than marijuana. *Arbitrary* isn't the right word, because all of this is an intentional part of carceral systems that give the power to use most medications only to doctors, along with the ability to incarcerate multiply marginalized disabled people at any time. Obviously legality is relevant in terms of strategizing, but morally, I refuse to let these laws define (or even influence) my own perceptions of right and wrong—and I suggest others do the same.

Drug Testing

Some doctors require drug testing (usually through urine screens) in order to get care. If your pee shows drugs in it that they didn't prescribe, then you are at risk of being kicked out of the practice. This can apply even to legal drugs or drugs prescribed by other doctors. In the small city where I live, there are only two practices that offer pain management, so one can easily lose total access to a myriad of services. This is especially fucked up because addictions can be related to under- or untreated pain.

Drug testing prevents someone from getting the health care they need. Doctors themselves will stress the importance of patients being forthcoming and honest so they can provide the best and most accurate health care. However, drug testing patients sets a tone of distrust that affects the entire doctor-patient relationship and undermines healing. The increased risk from greater surveillance is just because we are disabled and need medication or other treatment.

Drug Companies

Please don't mistake my enthusiasm for drugs as approval of the drug industry. Pharmaceutical companies cause so much harm to disabled people, including through the use of patents. Drug makers use intellectual property law to keep other companies from being able to replicate their medications. That means they can set whatever price they want, and people who can't afford it just can't get it, leading to unnecessary suffering and death.

The relationship between pharmaceutical companies and the carceral state is a reciprocal one. Sickness often gets you incarcerated, but healing only goes to those who can afford it. Healing should not be privatized, especially since our health depends on the health of those around us, as the COVID-19 pandemic has once again illustrated.

Self-Medication and Undertreated Pain

Many disabled people—but nowhere near all—deal with physical pain. Having unexplained pain was one of the first symptoms of my chronic illnesses, and I know a lot of other people who have been in pain with no "apparent" cause. Even when you have injuries or illnesses that happen to show up with the tools we have, doctors often don't believe patients who complain about pain, especially if you are not someone who presents as a white man with class and income privilege.

Pain management is political. Studies have shown that medical professionals believe that Black people have higher pain tolerances and thus are more likely to undertreat the pain of Black patients.[4] Whether pain is overtreated or undertreated will often depend on your race, ability, and access to insurance and your doctor's own biases.

Many people with disabilities don't require any kind of treatment or medication, but those of us who do are uniquely dependent on the medical system. However, a lot of disabled people can't get treatments for our disabilities due to lack of insurance or nearby providers, or treatments may not even exist. Poverty is a huge barrier to competent care. Even if you have public insurance, like Medicaid, it may not cover everything you need. The racism, ableism, fatphobia, sexism, and so on of the medical industry also alienates people from it, giving those in need of medication no other option but to treat themselves. This is often called "self-medication," but when that is your only option it's just "medication."

There are many people with pain, whether physical, emotional, or psychological, who can't get treatment for it legally. This could be because they don't have insurance, or because no one believes them, or because they don't have the ability to access the treatment. Thus, they may be forced to seek less legal means of pain control. It took me a long time, and I suffered a lot of trauma from the medical industry, before I was able to access pain management effective enough that I could even write this book. In the meantime, I had to figure it out on my own, which put me in situations that could have resulted in contact with the criminal justice system.

Overprescribing

While overmedication and undermedication may seem like opposites, they are actually two sides of the same coin. Doctors use the threat of addiction to keep some people away from necessary medication while simultaneously overprescribing other medications. By overprescribing I mean prescribing medications that an individual doesn't need or want. (What "need" and "want" mean in the context of the current system is an important question in itself, but not one I address here.)

People usually chalk up overprescribing solely to greedy drug companies. I don't want to let these murderous corporations off the hook, but that's only part of the story. Overmedication also serves a carceral purpose, and it is often used on people with cognitive and mental health disabilities to increase compliance in institutional settings. For example, one study found that older adults with intellectual disabilities were especially overprescribed psychotropic medications to help control their behavior.[5]

Overprescribing is one way the medical-industrial complex uses drugs carcerally, because these medications are not used for healing but to make it easier for the state to keep disabled people under control. Conversely, the denial of appropriate medication leads to behavior changes that put people at risk of being incarcerated or moved to even worse conditions.

For example, consider someone who takes psychiatric medication and is arrested and not given access to their medication, which causes increased mental health symptoms. Behavior then caused by lack of or improper medication allows the guards to move this person to solitary confinement, which further deteriorates their health. The lack of medical professionals in prisons and jails means that any potential prescriber will only have a brief time with the person whose symptoms have likely been unnecessarily increased by their environment. It's impossible under those circumstances for even the best and more well-intentioned doctors to accurately prescribe necessary medications. Prescribing improper medications or doses—whether too much, too little, or the wrong drug—are all signs of the same thing: a system that doesn't work for those who depend on it the most.

Forced Medication

As a matter of principle, no one should be medicated against their will. However, even in detox and rehab facilities, people are forced to take medication they don't want. Schenwar and Law make a similar point and also highlight how this especially affects disabled people:

> The point is not that medication is never useful or that science is unhelpful when it comes to mental health—medication often serves life-saving purposes. Instead, the question is one of consent, agency, and

self-determination. The person who will be using medication should make the decision whether to take it and under which circumstances. This is particularly important when it comes to heavy antipsychotic drugs that significantly alter the human experience for people diagnosed with "serious mental illness," often in ways that move them towards compliance with rigid social norms.[6]

Even beyond that, doctors in these facilities spend so little time talking to residents that they have no way to know what the proper medication would be. In one of the places I was in, I saw a doctor for a couple of minutes every few days at the most. Even then, one time he walked out of the room while I was talking. When I complained, one of the nurses told me not to take it personally and that the doctor just "doesn't listen to women." Situations like this are infuriating and traumatic, and in this case led to me being put on a medication that wasn't helpful.

Though there are laws around when and who can be forcefully medicated, in practice there isn't much you can do if you are incarcerated in any kind of facility. In *Insane*, Alisa Roth explains:

> There are many reasons that people may refuse psychotropic medications, even when they are medically indicated: an inability to recognize that one is sick, paranoia that the medication is poison, or simply not being able to handle the often severe side effects. Nevertheless, New York's statute allows for this bizarre distinction: "Misbehavior reports will not be issued to inmates with serious mental illness for refusing treatment, however an inmate may be subject to the disciplinary process for refusing to go to the location where treatment is provided or medication is dispensed." So you're free not to accept treatment, but you can still get in trouble if you don't show up for it.[7]

Changing a law or policy here and there won't ever lead to lasting change, because the state will find ways to work around it. That's another reason abolition is so important.

Mandatory Drug Treatment

Drug treatment is frequently forced on people with involvement in the criminal justice system. Sometimes they are given a "choice," but when the only other option is imprisonment, there is no real choice at all. Anything that is mandated and punishable by imprisonment is by definition carceral, so on that matter alone abolitionists should oppose forced treatment. A lot of well-intentioned people mistakenly think that being forced into treatment helps. It doesn't.

Mandated treatment doesn't even accomplish its stated goal of reducing addiction in any long-term way. Anyone who has personally experienced addiction knows that internal motivation is necessary (but not sufficient!—more on that below) for healing. A 2016 literature review published in the *International Journal of Drug Policy* looked at the effectiveness of compulsory treatment, and after reading all of the available literature the researchers concluded:

> Evidence does not, on the whole, suggest improved outcomes related to compulsory treatment approaches, with some studies suggesting potential harms. Given the potential for human rights abuses within compulsory treatment settings, non-compulsory treatment modalities should be prioritized by policymakers seeking to reduce drug-related harms.[8]

It's not just that mandatory treatment is useless and often harmful, it's also that the resources that are wasted could potentially have helped someone who did want the program. Forcing one group of marginalized people into a program that other groups of marginalized people are currently on waiting lists for doesn't make sense.

Differences in Facilities

The conditions in drug and alcohol treatment facilities vary wildly. People who can pay for treatment or have insurance coverage will often be allowed to choose where they go. This is not a privilege afforded to those without those resources. As disabled people are disproportionately poor, they are the ones more likely to be in more carceral facilities.

As I discussed in the last chapter, there is a huge difference in access to health care, based on whether someone has insurance and what kind they have. This is also true with drug treatment. Public insurance like Medicaid and Medicare will usually cover substance use treatment only in certain facilities—usually the same places where people who are mandated to drug treatment by the criminal courts are sent. Since the rules of these rehabs need to account for the kind of supervision required by the courts for mandated residents, voluntary residents who don't have access to private treatment are subject to the same conditions. While these facilities are not (usually) technically jails or prisons, that doesn't mean the conditions aren't sometimes similar. Some rehabs are considered worse than jail, and throughout my personal and professional experience, I've known more than a few people who chose jail over rehab when they were given the option. The more freedom a facility allows, the easier it is to stay there for the full mandated period without breaking the rules.

More than just taking up beds, the carceral approach has also affected the entire care profession, and treatment centers have become more like jails. In *Enforcing Freedom: Drug Courts, Therapeutic Communities, and the Intimacies of the State*, Kerwin Kaye wrote:

> The core elements within criminal justice–sponsored treatment programs concern waking up early, following orders ... learning bureaucratic procedures, and doing unpleasant, boring, and repetitive tasks without

complaint. Indeed, the need to do these tasks and obey all the rules is emphasized much more than any conventional counseling practice concerning drug use itself.[9]

Instead of research and innovation, resources are spent on holding people against their will. Once again, the drug treatment system is set up around the criminal justice system instead of healing.

Those who are mandated into treatment are also more vulnerable to coercion and control by staff members, since not completing treatment usually results in jail time. Therefore, leaving or being kicked out of these programs has carceral consequences in the most direct way. While in the criminal justice system these consequences come with at least lip service to accompanying rights, in treatment centers due process does not apply. Individual staff members are typically empowered to impose penalties on residents, including ones that can result in jail or prison time. These staff members may or may not have deescalation skills or know how to work with disabled people. This can lead to people with addictions paying the price for unskilled or inexperienced staff.

It's also not uncommon for treatment facilities to include harmful activities that sometimes rise to the level of abuse. Kaye saw residents forced to dig their own grave in one facility, which justified the activity by saying it was supposed to help residents understand that their drug use is killing them.[10] (In case it isn't obvious, further traumatizing people like this does not help them stay off drugs.)

The last issue with mandated treatment I will note here has to do with the way addiction services rely on the medical model and ignore the way external societal and structural conditions contribute to drug use. In other words, addiction is framed as an individual aberration that is "cured" through individual behavior. The problems that contribute to and exacerbate addiction, such as no access to decent medical care, poverty, and lack of stable housing, are not changed at all. The conditions that create addiction aren't addressed by these interventions.

Concurrent Disorders ("Dual Diagnosis")

The times that I was in inpatient facilities, I was in a unit for people with "dual diagnosis." This refers to people who have mental health disabilities and addiction issues, now usually called "concurrent disorders." These units are common, which you would think would lead to knowledge and innovations in treatment for disabled people. However, as a 2020 literature review of the best practices for the treatment of concurrent disorders shows, most facilities provide methods of treatment that we know don't work:

> The traditional approach in healthcare systems has been, and still is to address each issue separately, with limited or no standards to simultaneously address both components of concurrent disorder within the same care team. Traditional treatment methods of sequential or uncoordinated parallel care are nowadays considered obsolete. Despite new coordinated and integrated treatment approaches constituting the current standard, the majority of healthcare systems have yet to adapt.[11]

The researchers are saying that we know how to make these spaces more effective for disabled people with addictions, but we are not implementing them! In other words, many drug treatment spaces, especially mandated ones and those specifically for disabled people, are knowingly not using the best practices available. The reasons for and implications of this are myriad and woven throughout this book, but disabled people deserve the best treatment we can create, instead of systems intentionally making these places more carceral and using them as punishment.

This is especially galling because as people with "concurrent disorders," we need the most specialized treatment due to issues such as managing pain and addiction and the differences between physical dependence and addiction.

Addiction

Even though the current understanding of addiction is the disease model, which treats addiction as an illness, addiction is still usually punished carcerally. As noted above, most people who are incarcerated are there at least in part due to drugs. This includes the possession of drugs, behavior while intoxicated, and the homelessness and poverty that are sometimes consequences—and also causes—of addiction and significantly increase someone's chances of being arrested.

As society has moved toward using the disease model of addiction, the courts have implemented reforms for some people who have been determined to have addiction issues. While the specifics vary between programs, one thing that is consistent is that those who don't comply with the requirements of the program will be arrested. What this means practically is that often those who have the most advanced "disease" won't last long in treatment and are sent to jail or prison. The fear of jail is used to coerce people into rehab and to punish those who don't do what the court or facility employees want. These reforms admit that addiction should be considered an illness while simultaneously withholding treatment from the people who need it the most. There is no internal logic.

Drug Courts

Drug courts are another reformist reform that has led to increased incarceration, especially for disabled people. In *Prison by Any Other Name*, Schenwar and Law discuss how instead of shrinking the carceral system, drug courts strengthen it:

> Drug courts are also widening the net of control and surveillance: people who previously might have seen their charges dropped or been referred to voluntary

treatment are now often pressured by prosecutors, judges, and their own lawyers to plead guilty and enter court-mandated programs. Moreover, when drug courts are painted as the alternative, their punitive and harmful aspects are eclipsed.[12]

Drug courts are also seen as kinder and gentler than jail, but all it takes is one positive drug test or other misstep for the person to end up in jail, with likely a longer sentence than they would have had had they just pled guilty to begin with. Drug courts shrink the holes in the carceral net, which therefore catches more fish.

Participation in drug courts typically requires giving the state permission to test you for drugs and alcohol at any time. Programs differ, but many mandate regular attendance at court by participants, where they may be tested—and failing a test can lead to incarceration. Once again, though addiction is theoretically a disease, those most afflicted are punished the most harshly.

Kaye also notes the way drug courts reinforce racial differences at every step:

> In both their admission criteria (which favor the admission of white participants) and their procedural operations, drug courts provide a mechanism by which class and race privileged individuals who are caught up in the drug war might fairly consistently avoid the full penalty that was implicitly designed with the nonwhite poor in mind.[13]

Kaye is saying that even at their best, drug courts were designed as a sort of eject button from the criminal justice system for those who are privileged enough to be able to jump through the hoops that were created with a class-privileged white man who doesn't have disabilities (aside from their drug use) in mind. One way this is evident is the program's focus on employment, which automatically puts disabled people at a disadvantage, along with other marginalized people who are discriminated against.

As with mandated treatment, drug courts also don't do anything to improve the societal conditions that helped to create the addiction in the first place, and they place all the "blame" for addiction on the individual, practically if not theoretically.

Psychiatry

Many people consider psychiatry itself a carceral system. It's inarguably based on the medical model. It also treats mental illness as a disease to be cured, not just a different way of being in the world. A full critique of psychiatry from an abolitionist perspective is (say it with me) beyond the scope of this book, but critiques of psychiatry and the work of the antipsychiatry movement are crucial in examining the intersection of disability and carceral systems. Luckily for all of us, the antipsychiatry movement has produced a lot of great organizing and writing.

In *Psychiatry Disrupted: Theorizing Resistance and Crafting the (R)evolution*, Bonnie Burstow, a leader in the antipsychiatry movement, explains its aims:

> The goal of antipsychiatry is quite simple—nothing less than the abolition or end of the psychiatric system. Herein lies its ultimate distinction. While people critical of psychiatry but not fully antipsychiatry may take certain kinds of changes as sufficient—the advent of informed consent; less use of drugs; a kinder, gentler industry; or diagnostic categories that are less overlapping for example ... antipsychiatry holds that no changes will be sufficient, for the institution is too flawed and dangerous to simply be tinkered with.[14]

Psychiatry is a system that prescribes certain ways of being as "normal" and other ways of being as "abnormal." This is carceral, in that it marginalizes some people who are then criminalized. Psychiatry not only targets people, it also locks them up and drugs them. It also embodies the medical model by classifying mental illness as purely a biological "problem" to be chemically fixed.

The antipsychiatry movement is very involved in the fight for abolition and disability justice, and I am not giving it the proportional space it deserves, considering its prominence in these topics. However, the influences of the antipsychiatry movement, also called the "Mad Movement," can be seen throughout this book.

In *Call Me Crazy: Stories from the Mad Movement*, Irit Shimrat quotes Lanny Beckman, founder of Vancouver's Mental Patients Association, in 1970:

> I believe that there's no such thing as mental illness. But there's something wrong with some people. What's wrong with them is that they experience great amounts of pain and suffering. They may or may not be weird. If they're not weird they're called "neurotic." If they're weird they're called "psychotic." They're called "psychotic." They're called crazy: that's what "psychotic" means.
>
> I have a friend who was at the Queen Street Mental Health Centre in Toronto when she was sixteen. She recently got her records and gave them to me to read. There were 150 pages. They talked about her as if she were a machine. One note accused her of having an "immature personality." She was sixteen years old!
>
> One way of looking at psychiatry is that it's the medicalization of prejudice. And medicine is the secular religion of the age. So most people, when they see someone who is crazy or is in extreme and irrational pain—who has panic attacks or is too depressed to get out of bed for a month—say that that person is sick. They're mentally ill. There's something wrong with them and that "something wrong" is illness.[15]

While I agree with some of the general concepts and tenets of the antipsychiatry movement, I also have serious critiques. For example, sometimes antipsychiatry veers into healthism— prejudice against those who are unwell or different—and insistences that people are not sick, as if there is something wrong with being sick. Sickness isn't a moral value, it's just a descriptor, and there is nothing inherently wrong with it. Many times this is used to distance mental health from other aspects of the disability community, which often comes from inter- nalized ableism. As one of the principles of disability justice is solidarity across disabilities, this is especially important to keep in mind.

I also have found that for a lot of the people in my commu- nities, the issue isn't too much access to medications, but not enough or no access to the proper medications. This doesn't mean that we shouldn't also look at overmedicating ("both/ and"), but while the concerns of different communities do over- lap, they can also differ, depending on identity and access to resources.

Drugs under Abolition
Decriminalize Drugs

It doesn't have to be this way. Just as we know that the current drug policy causes harm, we know that the right changes to it can decrease harm. Eliminating the criminal penalties from drug use would do a lot to shrink the carceral state. Decriminalizing drugs is an abolitionist intervention that would also improve public safety and health. Derecka Purnell explains:

> Quality drug access and decriminalization could also prevent robberies and burglaries that can lead to murder and also undermine the conditions that lead to violence and police contact. Drug decriminaliza- tion permits people to exchange drugs more freely in private, public, and commercial settings. People might

be willing to ask for money they need for drugs instead
of stealing it.[16]

Criminalization of "illegal" drugs is inhumane, especially
based on what we know about drugs, addiction, and who is
arrested under these laws. Not only that, but it is incredibly
ineffective.

Harm Reduction

Luckily, there are things that we know do work to increase safety,
like harm reduction. Harm reduction was created by drug-using
and sex-working communities to keep themselves safe, because
they were abandoned by public health. The term *harm reduction*
has become more popularized, but it has also been co-opted
and neoliberalized—that is, privatized and run for the profit of
capitalists—instead of helping the most marginalized.

Lata Brooks and Mariame Kaba define harm reduction as:

> A philosophy of living, surviving, and resisting oppres-
> sion and violence that centers self-determination and
> non-condemning access to an array of options. Harm
> reduction is a set of practices that has been gifted to us
> by Queer and Transgender people of color, drug users,
> people in the sex trade and survivors of the HIV/AIDS
> epidemic. Harm reduction is not a public health inven-
> tion or a social work intervention, even though it has
> been used effectively in those fields.[17]

Harm reduction focuses on making things as safe as
possible for drug users and other marginalized people. This
includes needle exchange programs, supervised injection sites,
and other evolving strategies to keep people alive.

Access to the Right Drugs

As Purnell noted, one part of reducing harmful drug use that
is rarely considered is making sure that people have access to

the medications they need. This requires not only drugs but also diagnostic and other medical technology to understand more accurately what is going on. In other words, giving people the treatment they need, which includes time, respect, and resources, would reduce the need for people to self-medicate in ways that aren't healing.

Housing-First Policies

Everyone needs housing, but many people with addiction issues are not able to get housing assistance like Section 8 due to past criminal histories or penalties for being caught using drugs in their own home (even if those drugs are legal in the state where the person lives). To make matters even worse, many shelters and transitional housing programs require sobriety as a condition of admission to the program. These policies force substance users into the streets, putting them at risk of arrest at any time due to laws that criminalize homelessness, such as loitering laws.

Housing-first policies guarantee housing without conditions. It's impossible to focus on healing when you don't have safe and comfortable shelter, and these policies acknowledge that. These aren't laws (though they could be!) but rather practices of the organizations that provide (often government-funded) housing. As with any other policies we want, there are a number of approaches we can take here, such as advocating for existing organizations to change their policies around discharging participants for drug use, promoting the idea that funding go only to housing-first organizations, and creating (and enforcing) laws that don't allow organizations to discriminate on the basis of drug use.

Be Critical of "Treatment" and "Treatment Alternatives"

One of the consistent themes throughout this book is to always be suspicious when the state wants to take "care" of people. Just because something is called "treatment" doesn't necessarily mean there is anything healing about it. We always need to look closely, because "treatment" and "imprisonment" are frequently the same thing. (Literally, some treatment programs to which people are mandated involve jail stays.) Real treatment is not coercive and will respect self-determination and autonomy and focus on healing, not punishment.

This is not meant to be anywhere near a comprehensive look at drug policy and disabled people. I just wanted to point out a few of the important ways that drugs are used to lock up people who are disabled. It's crucial to understand that this happens not just through giving people too many drugs, but also through withholding necessary drugs, as well as the care necessary to accurately understand what is going on.

Though I focus a lot on individual access to treatment and services in this chapter, I want to be clear that drug use and misuse is a community issue and is intertwined with everything else, including disability.

Foundational Sources

Kaye, Kerwin. *Enforcing Freedom: Drug Courts, Therapeutic Communities, and the Intimacies of the State*. New York: Columbia University Press, 2020.

Schenwar, Maya, and Victoria Law. *Prison by Any Other Name: The Harmful Consequences of Popular Reforms*. New York: The New Press, 2020.

Social Work

Well-meaning people who are critical of incarceration and police will sometimes advocate replacing cops with social workers, but social work is also carceral—both conceptually, as a structure, and concretely, in the way the actions of social workers lead to incarceration. Many people enter the criminal justice system through or due to contact with social workers.

The information in this chapter largely comes from my own education and experience working in social work and adjacent fields. I got my bachelor's and master's degrees in social work and have worked in many different positions; the most relevant to this chapter involved spending a lot of time in family court. I've worked in "staff" and "managerial" positions, in large organizations and in small ones. I've been paid for my work (never fairly), and I've volunteered. All this to say, I know a lot about both governmental social services and the broader "social welfare" field.

What does this have to do with disability? I hope by this point it's obvious that everything involving systems involves disabled people, because disabled people are grossly overrepresented in these systems. Also, disabled people are uniquely reliant on social workers because we so often require benefits and care that necessitate engagement with the state. In other words, because disabled people are the ones interacting with social services the most, the carceral burden falls disproportionately on us. This is because the laws, policies, and underlying assumptions of the US social welfare system encourage and increase incarceration and other state control of multiply marginalized disabled people.

Who Is a Social Worker?

Before I dive in, I want to clarify a few things. First, I am using *social work* and *social worker* as broad terms that encompass many different titles and professions, and I'm using them very loosely. Generally, I'm thinking about situations in which one person is getting paid to help another person and in which the subtle or overt power dynamic is that the worker is assumed to have more social or institutional power than the client.

Because "social work" applies to such an array of people and organizations, some of these concepts will be more relevant than others in any given situation, and these nuances are important. To effectively strategize against all of the systems and structures that contribute to incarceration, we first need to understand them.

I'm writing this with the assumption that most people who go into the "helping professions" are well intentioned and invested in social change, like I was (and am). My critiques of the structure of social work and even of the actions of social workers aren't about individual social workers as people—though as I discuss below, there are things they can do to reduce their personal carceral impact—they are about the power that is bestowed to people in certain positions.

As Stefanie Lyn Kaufman-Mthimkhulu writes:

> Can social workers do good work in communities? Sure. But again, this is not about a few bad apples. This is about the pervasive and unrelenting nature of systemic racism, ableism, classism, etc.—and upholding the values of a white supremacist, cis heteropatriarchy. Social workers are operating under the same racist

and violent structures that are utilized to incarcerate, institutionalize, and strip freedoms away from Black and brown Americans.[1]

Part of the point of this chapter is to remind us that intentions are not enough. Just because we want to work toward liberation doesn't mean we won't accidentally end up causing harm. The solution to this isn't to turn inward and feel bad, but to learn more so we can do better.

Social Work Framework

The social work framework both mirrors carceral systems and helps to keep them in place. The general idea of social work is that there is a "professional" who "helps" another person. Inherent in this relationship is a power differential, with the worker having power that the client does not have. The sole function of many social workers is to gatekeep benefits or other resources, and they often end up having a lot of discretion in deciding who does and who doesn't get what they need.

Whereas the medical model identifies the problem in the individual, social work identifies the problem as something the individual has control over, which often isn't true. The purpose of social workers is usually to help someone make a change in their life—or assist them in jumping through one hoop or another. For example, if a social worker is assisting a client with obtaining employment, it doesn't matter how much the worker prepares them for the job interview if no one is willing to hire them—an unfortunately common thing for those with a criminal record and/or disabilities.

Social work is about helping people meet goals, but individual goals aren't helpful when the problem is society. Social work also doesn't question the underlying assumptions that the problem is the individual or something within the individual's control.

Of course, social work as a profession acknowledges social justice and oppression, but in practice it's about one educated (and often, though not always, white and nondisabled) person "helping" another person who usually has less societal power than them. The important part of the relationship in social work is that it doesn't disturb existing power relations.

Professionalization

"Professionalization" is the way that social workers separate themselves not only from their clients but also from the low-wage workers who often do most of the direct interfacing with clients in many organizations. Professionalization values credentials by gatekeeping education over experience, both lived experience and other experiences that occur outside of traditional organizations. This consolidates power in the most privileged, and as usual the most marginalized people's needs and perspectives are ignored.

The helping professions are overrun by white women, many of whom have never examined their own complicity in white supremacy and their other relationships to power. While obviously there are disabled social workers, disabled people are less likely to be able to access employment, especially more "professional" (i.e., powerful) roles. Of course, being disabled doesn't guarantee that someone will behave less oppressively or be less complicit in carceral systems, but the power differential between disabled clients and nondisabled workers adds another layer of difficulty for disabled individuals and communities.

The point isn't that we need more disabled social workers, but rather to illustrate the inherent power differential between social workers and their clients. Whether or not an individual social worker is disabled, if the laws and policies are ableist, then they will affect disabled people. That's why I'm focusing on policies that make a big difference in both preventing and responding to violence.

Social Workers as Judge

Social workers can be carceral in the most direct sense, in that they are empowered to send people to jail or prison. In some positions, social workers have a lot of the power of judges and courts, yet without the oversight. For example, many courts require being enrolled in certain programs (such as a halfway house program or a drug treatment program) as a prerequisite for people on parole or probation. Social workers are often the ones who make decisions about who is complying and who isn't. Usually, if an individual gets kicked out of the program to which they are mandated, they will end up back in jail or prison.

This may sound like a remote relationship, but in practice social workers frequently influence what happens in court through roles like determining whether someone has fulfilled certain court-imposed conditions or directly giving a report to the judge. One way that social workers have an especially negative impact on disabled children and adults is through the so-called child welfare system.

Child Protective Services Is Carceral

It goes by many names: child protective services, child and family services, the office of child and family services, child protection, and so on, but throughout the US, it serves the same function. I'm going to use the term *child protective services* (CPS) to refer to the parts of the government that are responsible for investigating child abuse and neglect and removing children from homes.

CPS is a major nexus between carceral systems and social services. While having a child removed from a family is not literal imprisonment, it's one of the few violations on par with being imprisoned. CPS also targets the same families that police and prisons do, and family separation is so intertwined with incarceration that termination of parental rights is a collateral consequence of many sentences, as I discuss below.

Like every other aspect of the carceral state, these policies disproportionately affect disabled people. Studies show that while only 9 percent of all children have a parent with a disability, 19 percent of those in foster care do.[2] Even the US Department of Justice has admitted that parents with a disability have been discriminated against and that the removal of children from disabled parents leads to long-term negative consequences for both parents and children.[3]

Carrie Ann Lucas (who I mentioned briefly in the chapter on health insurance) was a disabled parent and attorney who did a lot of advocacy around disabled parenting. Robyn Powell interviewed Lucas for an article about how unfair CPS is to disabled parents:

> Lucas is the mother of four children, all of whom also have disabilities. She has adopted each of them from foster care. Despite the state deeming her capable to adopt four times, Lucas has been referred to CPS on numerous occasions, and says she has "lost track" of the exact number.
>
> One time, for example, her daughter's school filed a report with CPS because the girl's ponytail was "too tight." Other times, Lucas was reported to CPS for neglecting her children because she wanted them to be independent and autonomous, such as requiring her teenage daughter to drive her own wheelchair from the school bus to the door of her home....
>
> It took a judge threatening to put the CPS worker in contempt of court if she didn't immediately place the child with Lucas. Lucas says the CPS worker told the judge, "There is no way that a handicapped woman can take care of a handicapped child. We're going to be picking up the child within two weeks."[4]

It's not just the personal biases of the people who work in what Dorothy Roberts calls the "family policing system," but also the laws themselves that make it easy for the children of disabled parents to be taken away.

Laws against Disabled Parenting

Removal of children solely because of their parents' disabilities is not an aberration; it is codified in many states. Thirty-five states include disability as a grounds for termination of parental rights.[5] Even those that don't have disability alone as a basis for removal include parental disability in the statutory list of things judges should consider when determining the best interests of children. These laws are discriminatory on their face. If the intention is to focus on the behavior of the parents and the care they provide, then that's what the laws should focus on, not a diagnostic label.

In a journal article that explains the importance of abolishing CPS, Robyn Powell shares another story about how these laws are used against disabled people:

> In Missouri, Erika Johnson and Blake Sinnett had their two-day-old daughter, Mikaela, placed in foster care because both parents were blind. Like many new mothers, Erika had trouble breastfeeding. Rather than assist the mother and daughter, a nurse reported the mother to a hospital social worker, setting into motion the family's involvement with the state's child protection services agency. Thereafter, social workers asked the parents a battery of questions about how they would care for Mikaela, which the parents answered in great detail. However, the one response they could not provide was that someone who was sighted would be with the newborn at all times. The parents could not afford such assistance, nor did they deem it necessary. A social worker subsequently informed the parents they would not be allowed to bring Mikaela home because the social worker could not "in good conscience send

this baby home with blind parents." During Mikaela's time in foster care, the parents were only granted supervised visits two to three hours per week. Mikaela was ultimately separated from her parents for 57 days.[6]

Blind people successfully parent all the time, and Mikaela only missed that important early parental bonding time because of the laws that allow CPS to remove children based on individual biases.

Poverty and "Neglect"

Those who haven't looked closely at the child welfare system are often under the impression that all the children who are removed from their parents have been severely abused. In fact, the vast majority of removals are due to "neglect." Obviously neglect isn't a good thing, as it means that the children aren't getting something they need. The problem is that "neglect" becomes a proxy for poverty. In Dorothy Roberts's book *Torn Apart: How the Child Welfare System Destroys Black Families— and How Abolition Can Build a Safer World*, Roberts writes:

> Only 16 percent of children enter foster care because they were physically or sexually abused. Child maltreatment is defined so as to detect deficits on the part of poor parents and to ignore middle-class and wealthy parents' failings.... The state punishes families because they are poor, not because they are dangerous.[7]

Anything that is a proxy for poverty will automatically have a huge effect on disabled people. Part of the problem, as I explain in the next chapter, is that US benefit policy forces disabled people to live in poverty. Though neglect statutes differ somewhat by state, they are all broadly written to encompass things that are either functions of poverty or are selectively enforced against the poor and disabled people of color that CPS focuses on. Many of the problems that lead to accusations of neglect, like lack of food or poor living conditions, are societal failures, not individual ones. Through neglect laws, CPS has license to remove children from the multiply marginalized families who have been victimized most by the economic policies of the US.

What so often ends up happening is that a disabled parent is poor and CPS gets involved as a "neglect" case, which ends up with the removal of the child. After the child is removed and placed in foster care, the government has to pay the foster parent to take care of the child. However, many times the only reason that the child was removed from their home in the first place was the original lack of resources. In other words, if the money that foster parents get can be given to biological parents instead, many fewer kids would be living in situations of "neglect" that make up the vast majority of CPS cases. While some states have laws that prohibit child removal solely on the basis of poverty, in practice—because being poor affects every aspect of someone's life and CPS and the court have so much discretion—it's impossible to enforce.

Further, since only the most extreme allegations of abuse come with criminal penalties, these cases are generally civil, so parents don't have the same constitutional and due process protections that people in criminal court have. In the 1981 case *Lassiter v. Department of Social Services*, the Supreme Court held that there is no federal requirement for family court to provide counsel to parents who are at risk of losing parental rights. Though some states have passed laws that require parents who can't afford a lawyer to be provided one, many parents face what may be the highest-stakes legal situation in their life without representation. This is especially a burden for the many parents who may have intellectual or other disabilities that make communicating in that environment especially difficult. Also, even when parents do have an attorney, that doesn't mean they are getting proper advocacy. When I had a job where I was in family court frequently, there were some great lawyers, but there also were many who had no clue (and weren't willing to learn) how to work with disabled clients. Many parents were afraid to talk to their own lawyers, in part because their experience with CPS was people pretending to be on their side and then fucking them over, and the lawyers would not take the time to explain the difference. Clients cannot meaningfully participate in their own defense if they don't understand this distinction.

Termination of Parental Rights and the ASFA

Termination of parental rights (TPR) is the legal severing of the relationship between the child and parent. TPR means that parents and children become "legal strangers" and thus parents cannot have court-enforced visitation rights or any other kind of access or decision-making power over the child. A Minnesota study found that disabled parents were more than three times more likely to have their parental rights terminated than parents without an identified disability.[8]

One of the policies that has increased TPRs, especially for disabled or incarcerated people, is the Adoptions and Safe Families Act (ASFA). The ASFA was signed into law in 1997, the year after welfare "reform" (which I don't even get into here but is an area that needs so much abolitionist organizing). The purpose of the ASFA is "family permanency," which it intends to accomplish by requiring the state to move for termination of parental rights if the child has been in foster care for fifteen out of twenty-two months.[9]

The ASFA's accelerated timeline puts a timer on parents and makes it much easier for the state to terminate parental rights. The fifteen months count not only the time a parent may actually need to get treatment or to resolve the issues that caused the removal in the first place, but also the time to convince the court of this and to comply with any requirements, which may take that long to begin with. For example, parenting classes are frequently mandated, but they may only be offered a few times a year.

This obviously has a huge effect on incarcerated people and gives the state yet another cudgel to beat criminalized populations with. Parents who are sentenced for fifteen months or longer are inherently at risk of permanently losing rights to their child *even in the absence of any kind of abuse or neglect.* In a Prison Policy Initiative article about these and other problems with the AFSA, Alison Walsh writes:

> In New York, for example, the median minimum sentence for women is 36 months—more than twice as long as the ASFA deadline. In 2008, almost 73% of women incarcerated in New York reported having one or more children. ASFA sets these mothers up to lose their children as soon as their sentences exceed 15 months. Loss of parental rights is almost always permanent and strips the parent of any right to know whether her child has been adopted, let alone to see her child.[10]

Permanency is theoretically a good thing, but what children have to give up for it—their family—is usually not worth it to the child or the parent.

The AFSA does provide some exceptions to the fifteen-month rule. The three exemptions are: if the child is in a relative's care and the state exercises the option, if the state thinks there is a documented "compelling reason," or if the state doesn't make "reasonable efforts" to provide necessary services to parents.[11] I would argue that none of the state's efforts are "reasonable," because what parents need are concrete resources like money and appropriate healthcare. In practice, these exceptions are very narrow. You may have noticed that every exception is based on the state's opinion of the situation or what the state provided, making them essentially nonexistent. While the state does have a lawyer, they usually get all (or at least most) of their information from the CPS worker, which gives them the power to frame the situation however they choose. Taking advantage of these exceptions also requires a lawyer, or at least legal knowledge well beyond the average parent.

A child's relationship with their biological parent(s) is vital and should only be severed in extreme situations. That doesn't mean every parent should or can parent full-time, but it does mean that preserving a relationship with a parent is something policies should encourage, not discourage. Since the ASFA was passed, even more studies have shown how important it is for children to keep a relationship with their biological parents in the vast majority of cases. Increasing termination of parental rights gets in the way of this relationship.[12]

TPRs are a huge deal, and as abolitionists we need to be on top of how and why the state uses these powers. (And everyone should read Dorothy Roberts!) The ASFA is just one of many policies that allows the state to control disabled people and keep us from having kids and parenting when and how we want.

Mandated Reporting

Another important link in the family separation chain is mandated reporting, because often that's how families end up on CPS's radar. Mandated reporting refers to laws and internal policies that require employees to contact the local child welfare office if they "suspect child abuse." I use quotes not because violence to children isn't real—it very much is—but because most people in mandated reporting roles don't know themselves what they should report. This is understandable, because even the laws don't define it well, which allows each individual "reporter" the ability to trigger state intervention in families with little to no guidance.

In the US, generally, anyone in a job involving any contact with children is a mandated reporter. This includes teachers, doctors, and staff members that work with youth. The specifics of the laws vary by location, but in my experience working across several states and organizations, whenever mandatory reporting issues came up it was always the same situation:

employees have a vague sense that they are mandated reporters, but they don't really know what it means or what to do, or even who to report to.

Being a mandated reporter doesn't require any specific kind of education or training, so the people making these decisions may not know anything about child abuse or take into account racism, ableism, and the other things that influence our determination of abuse. Mandated reporters may think they are helping when they call CPS, but they don't usually understand the trauma and hardship they may have put in motion.

Mandated Reporting Makes Kids Less Safe

In an article titled "Mandated Reporting: A Policy without Reason," Gary Melton explains that "experience has shown that the assumptions that guided the enactment of mandated reporting laws were largely erroneous."[13] One of these false assumptions is that "professionals"—who may or may not have had training on these topics—are in a good position to be able to identify children who are being abused.

In *Torn Apart*, Dorothy Roberts notes that teachers are both the professionals most likely to call CPS and the ones whose reports are the least likely to be substantiated.[14] The structures we have set up are not working.

Even if your only goal is to keep kids safe and you don't care about how many people are incarcerated, you should still be against mandated reporting, because it just doesn't work to reduce abuse. Studies have found that mandated reporting laws are affirmatively harmful to children.[15] Beyond the ways they increase state violence to families through CPS, mandated reporting laws also are harmful because they make children less likely to tell people outside the family about abuse, because they are afraid of removal. These laws also keep parents from being able to be open with the people they are supposed to get help from (like social workers).

Keeping Children Safe from Family Separation

So what do you do if you are a mandated reporter and suspect abuse? Here are some ideas and jumping-off points. As always, communities themselves are the only ones who can know what will work best to take care of each other, and this issue cannot be addressed in isolation. Below are some things to think about that I have used to help problem-solve with people who are in this position. The underlying question we are trying to answer is: What can we do that will *actually* help?

Is There Abuse?

The first step is to identify what makes you suspect abuse. Many times circumstances that are just different from the way we do things may seem harmful, but aren't. Especially consider the way oppression may play into the situation. We do this not so we can ignore abuse when marginalization is at play, but to fully understand the situation to better be able to be of real help. If after unpacking your own biases and perspective you feel like there is abuse going on, getting your thoughts concrete can be helpful to figure out what to do next.

What Does the Kid Need?

As I noted above, the vast majority of cases of child abuse are related to neglect, which is usually related to poverty. A lot of problems can be solved by resources, and a lot of problems are created by the systems that distribute those resources. Abolition is about giving people what they need instead of punishing them for what they don't have. The amount and kind of resources available in any situation will vary and will almost never be enough, but with creative thinking you may be able to figure out something that will be helpful.

Fuck Your License

What makes a mandated reporter a mandated reporter is that if they don't report abuse, they could theoretically lose their job or their professional license. However, in practice there is rarely any real risk, because it's almost always speculative to begin with. Even CPS workers themselves—who have a much higher legal responsibility in these scenarios than most mandated reporters—rarely face consequences for not alerting others to unconfirmed abuse. Even if not reporting could mean losing a job, reporting can ruin lives.

I'm not saying do nothing if you suspect abuse or neglect. I'm saying the opposite: do what you need to do to actually help the child and family, not to create more problems for them. If you are in a professional role, understand that you have so much power over that person and if you are wrong or mistaken, you could cause extreme trauma and open the door to state involvement.

Each situation is unique, and I'm not prescribing any specific behavior necessarily, except being thoughtful about the true consequences of our actions, whether we are concerned in a professional or personal situation.

Aja D. Reynolds wrote about how the organization Black Girl Free (BGF) approached the issue of mandatory reporting:

> Although BGF is built upon abolitionist principles, we are beholden to mandated reporter standards in reporting any child abuse to state agencies that often rely on carceral interventions. We often have to leverage resources and support in assisting our young people from other agencies and organizations complicit in these practices as well. This has meant building strong relationships with allies in those spaces and engaging our girls' networks of supports that include family, friends, partners, teachers, and others they identify as assets in their lives. It is from within these relationships that we are able to navigate institutions in ways that uphold the agency of our young people and our own organizational values. These engagements have also

given us the opportunity to educate about and advocate for processes in service to Black girls.

In one instance where a young person was experiencing neglect from a parent, we were able to work with the principal at the young person's school to create a short-term and long-term plan to intervene. Unlike many child welfare agencies, we engaged the parent from a place of love rather than judgment to learn more about issues in the home and worked with the family to address the financial needs that impeded the parent's ability to prioritize other direct needs of their children.[16]

I think most mandated reporters contact authorities not only because they have a professional responsibility to do so but also because they think it will help the child. However, these systems end up harming children, especially the most vulnerable ones, including disabled kids and those with disabled parents.

CPS doesn't just disproportionately impact disabled parents. Disabled children are overrepresented in the child welfare system and foster care.[17] When children are taken from their parents, the risk of abuse goes up. When disabled kids are removed from their parents, they also tend to spend a longer time in foster care, due to the lack of foster parents willing to adopt a disabled child. For the same reason, they are also more likely to be put in an institution. The child welfare system implicates much about disability, and we need to understand this link in order to understand the best way to actually keep families safe.

Abolishing CPS

Abolishing CPS doesn't excuse abuse or neglect, but rather it takes a research-based approach to what keeps families safest. Though we currently frame neglect as a parenting issue, it could just as easily be considered a societal failure. These are important needs, and as a society we owe it to all our kids to help these needs be met.

While income is not supposed to be taken into account when removing children from their parents, proxies for income can be. For example, if a parent cannot afford safe housing, then their child may be taken away. It would make much more sense and be more humane to give that parent the money they need for suitable housing instead of paying even more money to remove the child and put them in foster care.

If these systems were actually concerned about children in this country not having what they need, they would focus on providing it to families instead of separating them. Roberts writes: "The most successful approach would be to invest in the things that have been proven to promote child's well-being: a living wage and income supports for parents; high quality housing, nutrition, education, child care, and health care; freedom from state and private violence; and a clean environment."[18]

Importantly, this support cannot come from the same person who can take your child away! If we want to make meaningful changes in families and prevent abuse and neglect, we have a lot of different strategies we can use.

Most people want to be good parents and try their best to parent. They just may need help, and that help may not be something that even currently exists—but that doesn't mean it can't. For cases that are more extreme and intense, we can create resources that go into depth to handle those situations.

I want to end this chapter with a quote from Emma Peyton Williams in "Thinking Beyond 'Counselors, Not Cops'": "What if, instead of accepting the model of safety that is handed down by police and family regulation caseworkers alike, we thought critically about what safety would look like to us? What if we condemned family separation of all sorts, naming family separation as a safety risk to everyone involved?"[19]

Foundational Sources

Education for Liberation Network & Critical Resistance Editorial Collective, ed. *Lessons in Liberation: An Abolitionist Toolkit for Educators.* Chico, CA: AK Press, 2021.

Roberts, Dorothy. *Shattered Bonds: The Color of Child Welfare.* New York: Basic Books, 2002.

Roberts, Dorothy. *Torn Apart: How the Child Welfare System Destroys Black Families—and How Abolition Can Build a Safer World.* New York: Basic Books, 2022.

Benefits and Charity

Though the stated rationale of benefit programs is to help people, they are structured to be part of the carceral framework. To put it simply: prisons are the stick and benefits are the carrot. The chapter on health care showed how access to benefits can determine life or death, yet they don't get the attention they deserve by the left. Partially it's because benefits are less sexy than protesting in the street, but being able to connect someone to benefits can be lifesaving, and changing benefit policy would have a huge impact on incarceration. It's crucial that we understand the way these systems work, whether we are fighting within them or against them.

The benefit scheme in the US shows who is valued (and who isn't), and it explains why so many disabled people are poor. This is just an overview, and I try not to get too into the weeds, but both my social work and legal training involves benefit policy, so it is a special area of interest for me. Here, I try to focus on just some of the more common benefits disabled people may have access to.

How Are Benefits Carceral?

Before I get into the specifics of benefit policy, I want to discuss how benefits connect to incarceration. The current benefits system is carceral because it restricts freedom by invading privacy, and increased surveillance will always lead to increased incarceration. The way benefits are set up is also carceral, because they are so difficult to get, and the amounts are so paltry, that applicants are required to participate in crim-inalized or gray-market economies to get by.

Because there is such a direct relationship between poverty and incarceration, access to money inherently equals access to freedom.[1] In most jurisdictions, judges have the ability to require bail before they will release an arrestee. Bernadette Rabuy and Daniel Kopf published a study with the Prison Policy Institute that looked at how "money bail perpetuates an endless cycle of poverty and jail time."[2] They noted that a typical bail amount is $10,000, an amount so out of reach for many of the people arrested it may as well be a billion dollars. They wrote:

> Examining the median pre-incarceration incomes of people in jail makes it clear that the system of money bail is set up so that it fails: the ability to pay a bail bond is impossible for too many of the people expected to pay it. In fact, the typical Black man, Black woman, and Hispanic woman detained for failure to pay a bail bond were living below the poverty line before incar-ceration. The income data reveals just how unrealistic it is to expect defendants to be able to quickly patch together $10,000, or a portion thereof, for a bail bond. The median bail bond amount in this country repre-sents eight months of income for the typical detained defendant.[3]

While a bail bond only requires a percentage of the total amount to secure release, the money is nonrefundable. This takes money out of the pockets of the communities that need it most.

The cash bail system incarcerates people who don't have the personal or community resources to secure their freedom, something disabled people are especially likely to experience. A 2012 study by the Council of State Governments looked at New York City courts and found:

Individuals with mental illnesses were less likely to make bail and stayed in jail considerably longer before making bail. The majority of admissions (80 percent) to DOC were pretrial detainees who had bail set but were not able to make bail at arraignment. While people with mental illnesses admitted to DOC had minimum bail amounts set that were comparable to those without mental illnesses, only about 12 percent of individuals with mental illnesses made bail post admission, compared to about 21 percent of those without mental illnesses. Furthermore, people with mental illnesses took five times as long to make bail as those without mental illnesses (48 days vs. 9 days).[4]

The cash bail system unfairly burdens disabled people, and access to resources reduces the personal impact of carceral systems. Even though disability benefits are (at this moment) unconscionably paltry, those without access are even worse off.

The way benefits are structured can increase (or decrease) the breadth and depth of the carceral state. In a general sense, because of the relationship between poverty and incarceration, the stronger the "social safety net," the less incarceration. The more accessible and livable disability benefits are, the less disabled people need to do things that could get them arrested to make ends meet or be forced into the criminal justice system in another way.

Disability Benefits

There are several different kinds of government resources someone may be able to access because of their status as a disabled person. This includes things like discount public transportation, heating assistance, and food stamps. But in the US when people talk about "disability benefits," what they usually mean are Supplemental Security Income (SSI) and Social Security Disability Insurance (SSDI). (Don't worry yet about the distinction between the two programs—I go into that later.) These programs pay monthly benefits to those who are deemed disabled.

SSI and SSDI are both federal programs, which means the laws and regulations are consistent throughout the US. Though different circuits have different case law, generally the requirements are the same in every state. When I was a lawyer, a couple of the jobs I had involved writing SSI and SSDI appeal briefs, which required knowing a lot about these laws. I'm saying this as a warning that I'm about to go pretty deep into the structure of these programs and what the similarities and differences between them mean, but I'll try to make it understandable, because it's illuminating both conceptually and in practice. I've also tried to access benefits myself and have experienced the system from that side. It is a nightmare, but more for some people than others.

Eligibility

Note that it's not the disability itself that grants benefits, but the government designation as a disabled person, which is why looking at eligibility is so important. Any potential or existing policy that's restricted to disabled people necessarily has to draw a line between who is disabled and who is not, and abolitionists can (generally) push for that line to be as inclusive as possible for benefits.

In "Medieval Poor Law in Twentieth Century America: Looking Back towards a General Theory of American Poor Relief," Larry Cata Baker addresses the way eligibility has always been used as a means of control:

> Poor relief manipulates need by imposing queuing requirements on the destitute. Queuing, serving as the means of distributing limited resources, takes two primary forms: discrimination based on impermanent eligibility criteria, and shifting definitions of hierarchies

of need. By fine-tuning these forms of queuing, stasis reinforces the societal belief that not everyone in need is needy enough to be supported by other than his or her own efforts. Further, manipulation serves to enforce the cultural norm (obligation) to fend for oneself. Adjusting the definition of eligibility and need can also effectively "punish" deviance from accepted cultural mores and reinforce the established social order. Because the definition of need is a moving target, qualifying at one time does not guarantee continuing qualification.[5]

Even from the very beginning these systems used changing eligibility as a way to strategically include or exclude people from benefits they need. People who need benefits have to comply with requirements, thus limiting their freedom.

Similarities between SSI and SSDI

While there is a lot that is different about SSI and SSDI, the general body of statutes case law is exactly the same. So, adults have to prove the same thing for both of them in terms of disability, that they are "unable to engage in any substantial gainful activity by reason of any medically determinable physical or mental impairment which can be expected to result in death or which has lasted or can be expected to last for a continuous period of not less than twelve months."[6] This is proven through medical records and (theoretically) the testimony of the applicant. (Though there are laws that address how much weight an applicant's testimony should be given, in practice the administrative law judge doesn't have to give any credibility to the testimony.)

So you not only need to be disabled, you need to prove disability. Being disabled isn't enough; you need to have medical records that show you are disabled. This may be obvious, but the consequences of requiring medical records isn't often considered. Getting the medical evidence to qualify for disability benefits is especially hard for the people most likely to be disabled: people without access to medical care.

Another issue with needing medical records to get SSI and SSDI is that individuals who have spent a lot of time in jail and prison don't have substantial medical records, because the treatment in jails and prisons is so bad. So what I have seen happen many times is that someone ends up in jail or prison because of their disabilities, but during that time they do not necessarily have documentation of being disabled. Then, when they go home and are too disabled to work, they can't get benefits, because they don't have the medical records. This once again forces people into criminalized economies, poverty, and/ or homelessness, which then puts them back in jail or prison, and the cycle continues.

So no matter how disabled you are, if you don't have records that convincingly prove your disability—even if those records would be impossible to get or just don't exist—you cannot get disability benefits. The benefit system is built to exclude people, even people who qualify. Almost everyone gets automatically rejected on their first application and has to go through the appeals process, no matter what their record shows. This makes the process frequently take years.

Even after an individual has been determined to be disabled, there is a five-month waiting period before benefits can begin. I do not know how anyone expects disabled people to live in the interim when by these programs' own requirements they can't work substantially. It's not a safety net if you have to hit the ground first.

SSDI versus SSI

Social Security law literally splits disabled people into categories that mirror the Elizabethan Poor Laws' separation of "deserving" (SSDI) and "undeserving" (SSI) poor. The "undeserving" are forced by the system's own rules to live in extreme poverty for the rest of their lives, while the "deserving" get to live in slightly less abject poverty. (One way to remember the difference is that the one with more letters—SSDI—gives slightly more benefits, as I discuss below.) The way that SSI and SSDI are set up hinges worthiness on the ability to participate in capitalism.

Though the two programs define disability the same way and you have to prove the same thing, there are other eligibility requirements that are different that distinguish SSI and SSDI from each other. SSDI requires recipients to have worked for a certain amount of time or made a certain amount of money before they became too disabled to work. So, if you have been too disabled to work your entire life, you will not qualify for SSDI.

Conversely, you can be eligible for SSI even if you have never worked before. So, if you have not worked enough to be eligible for SSDI, then the only other option for disability benefits is SSI.

Benefit Amounts

SSI and SSDI also pay different benefit amounts, with SSDI paying more. In 2022, the maximum monthly individual benefit amount was $841 for SSI and $3,345 for SSDI. Few people receiving SSDI get the maximum, and the average benefit amount for SSDI in 2022 was $1,358. Essentially, the government forces people in the US who are born disabled and can't work to spend their whole lives in poverty (unless they happen to have family or other resources, which of course a lot of us don't). If you are able to work at some point, then your benefits will be proportional to the amount of money you made while you were working.

Some may argue that these two systems have different rationales: SSDI is supposed to be more like insurance, where you pay while you work and if you can't anymore then you can get benefits out of that "pool" of money, whereas SSI is an entitlement program that anyone can get if they meet certain income and disability criteria, and so the money is "public" money. While this is true, it doesn't change anything.

We understand disability as something that someone doesn't have control over, yet we penalize people for being disabled at a younger age.

SSDI Puts the "Poor" in Deserving Poor

While it's definitely better to be considered "deserving," unless they have other income or resources, even those who can get SSDI benefits are forced to live in poverty (or near poverty) for the rest of their lives. Therefore, unless they have access to other resources, disabled people who can't work have no other choice but to be poor.

Income Limits

Another big difference between SSI and SSDI is that SSI is means tested. Means testing is a process that determines that you are only eligible for benefits if you make below a certain amount of money. This may seem like a good idea, because theoretically we want to keep benefits for the people who are the poorest and need them the most. However, means testing automatically disqualifies some people who need the benefits, whether because of income that is slightly over the threshold, an inability to get necessary documentation, or any of the number of other reasons people who may theoretically be eligible for benefits don't get them. Any kind of requirement will screen out some people who genuinely need the benefit. Also, implementing means testing costs money that could be given directly to people.

SSI and SSDI both require recipients to prove that they are too disabled to work at a level of "substantial gainful activity." Beneficiaries are allowed to work a little bit if they are able, but after a certain level of earned income, benefits will be reduced or taken away, and SSI starts penalizing benefits before SSDI does. The specifics are complicated, but SSI will reduce benefits with even a small amount of work, while SSDI allows recipients to earn more before cutting benefits.

Asset Limits

Another critical difference between the programs is that SSI has asset limits and SSDI doesn't. While means testing has to do with the amount of income that is coming in in any given month, asset limits have to do with how much someone has. In 2022, the SSI asset limits were only $2,000 for individuals and $3,000 for couples.[7] This means single people cannot have more than $2,000 in the bank without losing eligibility for SSI. These amounts are disgustingly low. Keep in mind that being disabled is more expensive than not being disabled. Even if someone is able to find the money, SSI doesn't let people save money for future expenses over $2,000, which means that pretty much any emergency will turn into a crisis.

What Is Counted

SSI and SSDI also differ in whose and what income is counted. SSI counts the whole family's income, while SSDI only looks at individual earned income. Because SSDI only focuses on how much someone can work, it doesn't count spousal income or "unearned" income, such as interest. SSI looks at the income and assets of married couples together, and thus many disabled people cannot get married without losing their benefits.

Section 8

The benefit system is also carceral in the way it expands surveillance on people who receive benefits, therefore making it more likely they will be arrested for the same things that richer, whiter, and more abled people do in the same proportions. Section 8 is a US housing voucher program for people who are disabled, elder, or very poor. It pays all or part of the rent for those who qualify and who are able to find housing that accepts Section 8. This second part is harder than it may seem, since many landlords refuse to take Section 8, even though it is one of the most secure ways to guarantee that rent is being paid each month, because it is being paid by the government. Even beyond finding someone who accepts Section 8, the housing market is much narrower for disabled people who need accessible housing, which can make finding housing almost impossible. Further, in order to get Section 8 vouchers, you need to get on a usually very long waiting list that is open at sporadic times, making it all incredibly confusing and difficult to access.

People who rely on Section 8 are not allowed to have family or friends stay with them and are also forced to endure intrusive "inspections," in which their houses are searched. I talked to my friend Lanah after a Section 8 inspection, who explained the process: "The inspectors went through every drawer. They say it's to 'make sure the drawers work,' but really it's so they can search for drugs and see if there are other people living there."

Besides meeting the eligibility requirements, being on Section 8 also requires abandoning all dignity and privacy. It means having strangers come into your house and go through all your stuff. It also means always being worried about your housing being taken away at any time and never being able to get comfortable even in your own home.

It's not as if Section 8 allows for reasonable living arrangements either. Lanah is forced to share a room with her disabled mom, because Section 8 thinks that two bedrooms is enough for two adults and two children. (Note that CPS in some places could have a problem with this same arrangement, forcing people into impossible situations.)

With all these conditions, it's impossible to relax. The stress this creates can't be underestimated. As Lanah said: "People want Section 8 for the rent, which is great . . . but baby, it isn't worth my dignity. I'm tired."

Section 8 is a good example of just how much people have to give up to get the "benefits" they are entitled to. Just by virtue of being disabled and needing help, Lanah and others need to give up their privacy. Though the extent and type varies by benefit, jurisdiction, and other factors, including an individual social worker's mood, even benefits that are considered "entitlements" include some kind of surveillance or monitoring. And, as discussed throughout this book, the more anyone is watched, the more likely they are to get into trouble.

Many disabled people are also ineligible for Section 8 due to criminal history. Federal law bars those convicted of certain crimes from receiving Section 8, which makes it hard for disabled people with records to find safe housing, and many end up homeless or in unsafe situations.

The system keeps disabled people in poverty with no or few choices but to participate in criminalized activities, which then makes them ineligible for necessary housing services. This then makes it even harder for them to get by and more likely that they will end up in jail or institutions. Safe and accessible (including affordable!) housing is necessary for everyone, and those without it face a huge risk of incarceration. Housing that has requirements and strings attached (whether a clear criminal record or sobriety or invasive inspections) is carceral.

Abolitionist Benefit Reforms

Throughout this chapter I have identified many problems with benefits, but there are tons more. On the bright side, this means there are a lot of opportunities for abolitionist-influenced campaigns. For example, if the asset limit for SSI were eliminated (or even just increased, as has been proposed recently), it would have a huge impact. Of course, this would not change the structure of the system, but it could help to keep some people a little further from criminalization's clutches.

Benefit reforms may not be what people think of when they think of abolition, but this is actually a fertile ground for abolitionist organizing. As with all policies, the specifics are important, but abolitionists need to be part of the conversation.

By definition, people on SSI are poor and disabled, the exact people most affected by carceral systems. (Not all poor and disabled people are on SSI, but all of the people on SSI are poor and disabled.) Raising benefit amounts is one way for more money to go to people who have been criminalized because of their poverty. If benefits can be carceral, they can also be abolitionist.

The NPIC

I first learned about the concept of the nonprofit industrial complex (NPIC) through the work of Incite! Women of Color against Violence, specifically their wonderful book *The Revolution Will Not Be Funded: Beyond the Non-profit Industrial Complex*, and this section is heavily indebted to that groundbreaking anthology. In it, Dylan Rodríguez defines the NPIC as "the industrialized incorporation of pro-state liberal and progressive campaigns and movements into a spectrum of government-proctored non-profit organization."[8] In other words, a web of public and private institutions, policies, and relationships that reinforce the coercive neoliberal values of capitalism.

The NPIC's relationship to liberation is similar to that of (mainstream) social workers. They both appear to make changes while really upholding the status quo and dampening social movements. This is pernicious in the way it neutralizes liberation movements and waters down organizer demands. Rodríguez explains: "The NPIC's (and by extension the establishment Left's) commitment to *maintaining* the essential social and political structures of civil society (meaning institutions, as well as ways of thinking) reproduces and enables the most vicious and insidious forms of state and state-sanctioned oppression and repression."[9]

The NPIC obfuscates the actual cause of the problems—like the structures that I talk about in this book—and funnels all the resources into things that don't address the root causes of the issues and often make things worse.

It's like the parable where two men are walking by a river and notice that babies are floating in it. One man immediately jumps into the water to start rescuing babies, and the other keeps walking. The one who dove in sees what he thinks is his friend being cruel and yells to ask him where he is going. The friend answers, "I'm going to see who's throwing the babies in the river." The point being that it's easier to stop something at the source. Even at their best, the most nonprofits can be is the man who immediately jumps into the river. Typically, they either just walk by without doing anything or, often, are the ones throwing the babies in.

Even on its face, all the NPIC does is offer Band-Aids, because nonprofits can't disrupt the state when they inherently require being sanctioned by it. "Nonprofit" is a specific status that is granted by the government to corporations that have been incorporated under section 501(c) of the tax code. Though there are theoretically laws governing what kind of activities these corporations can take part in, they are rarely enforced once status is granted. Even assuming the laws were followed to the letter, the structure of this system is inherently incompatible with disrupting the state, because it depends on state favor.

The NPIC acts as a mechanism for the upward transfer of wealth. Being recognized as a nonprofit allows these organizations to not pay taxes on their income, which funnels money that is supposed to be public into the private hands of nonprofits. Further, nonprofit status also allows donations to them to be tax-deductible, which gives tax benefits to donors—once again removing resources from public hands. This not only diverts resources away from the public, but also trains us to expect less from the money that the government does hold on to.

When we expect less, it keeps us from holding the government's feet to the fire. Christine Ahn's essay in *The Revolution Will Not Be Funded* explains the way the charity model shapes the government's role in the public imagination: "Many Americans are seduced by the idea that piecemeal voluntary efforts can somehow replace a systematic public approach to eliminating poverty. But this reasoning is based on the inherent falsehood that scarcity—rather than inequality—is at the root of these persisting social and economic problems."[10]

This reinforces the myth of poverty as an individual failure instead of an intentionally created class of people.

Another function of the NPIC is to shift the burden of taking care of people from the government to private nonprofits and the religious sector. For example, the Wounded Warrior Project (WWP) is a 501(c)3 that assists veterans who were disabled in the US military after September 11, 2001, including services related to mental and physical health. According to its 2022 annual report, the WWP spent $247 million on programs for veterans.[11]

Circularly, one of the things the WWP does is to help individual clients get VA benefits. While it's true that veterans do often need assistance to access benefits, but imagine if that $200 million was invested in ensuring fewer barriers to VA benefits instead of paying more privileged people to act as liaisons between those in need and the resources they are entitled to? This sounds good until you realize that it is duplicating services that are supposed to be provided by the Department of Veterans Affairs (VA), which requested $269.9 billion in fiscal year 2022.

The NPIC's own work is hurting the communities it is purported to serve. Instead of holding the government's feet to the fire, nonprofits let it off the hook in providing even the most basic of things. Because nonprofits rely on the state, they can't challenge it.

Working Outside the NPIC—Mutual Aid

Luckily, there are lots of ways to work outside the NPIC. Mutual aid is one framework. Instead of professionals coming into communities and "helping," mutual aid is community members working together as both people who give and people who receive care. In *Mutual Aid: Building Solidarity during This Crisis (and the Next)*, Dean Spade defines mutual aid as "collective coordination to meet each other's needs, usually from an awareness that the systems we have in place are not going to meet them."[12] Mutual aid is in direct contradiction to a model where a privileged professional coerces someone with less power to do things that won't likely end in real change.

Spade identifies three important elements of mutual aid projects. First, mutual aid projects "work to meet survival needs and build shared understanding about why people do not have what they need."[13] Mutual aid has an overtly political component that seeks to understand the root cause of the issue, which is an important difference between mutual aid and social work. While social work does acknowledge that there is injustice, the profession is primarily based on helping individuals—not policy—to change. Mutual aid projects are focused on mobilizing people, expanding solidarity, and building movements. In other words, mutual aid focuses on changing the systems that caused the need in the first place.

Finally, mutual aid projects are participatory, which means that they are accomplished by the communities they serve, not by an outside "savior." This is the exact opposite of the dynamic between a helping professional and client, in which the client is purposely disempowered by the system and forced to jump through whatever hoops the professionals and systems decide to create. Mutual aid is about us helping ourselves and understanding that we have what we need if we can organize.

I am not saying that nonprofits have never done work that contributes to abolition, and I'm not (necessarily) saying that organizations should never be nonprofits. It may be the most strategic way to move forward considering the material realities. Though I may have opinions, the cost-benefit analysis is for the people most directly affected in any situation to consider. However, we need to be strategic and thoughtful about the choices we make as well as all of the consequences of those choices, especially on those who have less power than us.

The NPIC is a wolf in sheep's clothing. (Or a capitalist in socialist's clothing?) We need to understand that seemingly good intentions are not enough, and we need to look closely at the actual consequences of the current structure.

Foundational Sources

Incite! Women of Color against Violence, ed. *The Revolution Will Not Be Funded: Beyond the Non-profit Industrial Complex*. Cambridge, MA: South End Press, 2007.

Spade, Dean. *Mutual Aid: Building Solidarity during This Crisis (and the Next)*. London: Verso, 2020.

Disablement

Carceral systems both penalize and weaponize disability. The state doesn't just target disabled people, the state literally disables people. I use the word *disablement* to refer to state-caused disability, whether directly or indirectly.

Disability on its own isn't a bad thing, but illness and harms caused by poverty and oppression are. While this requires a little nuance, I don't think it's too hard to understand how we can prevent not disability itself, but the pain and sickness that may lead to disability, while simultaneously celebrating disabled people and bodies. This is not comprehensive, nor is it detailed, but I wanted to note some of the common ways that disablement works.

In a country where disabled people are stripped of rights, the state can use disablement as a way to gain control over individuals, whether through rationales of "care" or "danger." Disability is sometimes used as a pretext for a white supremacist agenda, which is why it's so important to look at how disability is racialized, especially the relationship between Blackness and disability. More simply: if the state has power over disabled people, all it needs to control someone is to make them disabled. It does so by defining Blackness as inherently disabled, and also by literally sickening marginalized people through lack of health care, criminalized prenatal care, CPS, the things I talk about in this chapter, and so much more.

Jails, Prisons, and Institutionalization
Jails, prisons, and other institutions themselves are disabling.

If someone is not disabled before they get there, they will be soon after. Just as the police don't stop violence but rather cause violence, institutionalization (of all kinds) doesn't heal people, it disables them. Between the lack of medical care in most institutional environments and the universally terrible food, institutions are not places where it is possible to maintain health, even if you come in healthy. Their whole environment is meant to destabilize and traumatize.

It's not just the individual who is disabled by these environments, but also their children. The prison- and medical-industrial complexes destroy whole communities, and the harm is felt for generations. In *Policing the Womb*, Michele Goodwin noted, "Children who experience parental incarceration suffer greater harms related to attention deficit, behavior or conduct problems, language and articulation challenges, and developmental delays than children who experience parental divorce or parental death."[1]

Having a family member incarcerated is related to increased stress and other matters that affect health and ability. Incarceration is also extremely traumatic, and as I explain below, trauma is disabling.

Poverty and Homelessness

One running thread through this book is the connection between poverty and disability. In *Becoming Abolitionists*, Derecka Purnell wrote:

> At Harvard, wealth was displayed through coats, cuffs, Chanel bags, number of homes, and investments. But the students' and professors' bodies conveyed wealth, too. It bought insurance, nannies, access to clean air, and more time to live. My grandmother was in a fetid elderly facility; my wealthy white professors her age still lectured.[2]

If someone is poor enough, they are essentially certain to

become disabled, especially if they are homeless for any period of time. According to Liat Ben-Moshe:

> Homelessness by itself disables. The streets, or shelters or living day to day without housing security are disabling psychologically as well as physically. The constant noise, diesel fumes, cold/heat, lack of privacy, anxiety of not knowing where the next meal will come from, fear of attack, and fear of being removed or arrested by police are part and parcel of everyday living without permanent shelter.[3]

The fact that people in this country don't have a right to shelter even though there is plenty is one of the ways that the state enacts disablement.

Dangerous Jobs

Another reason that marginalized people tend to become disabled is because they are forced into dangerous jobs (including criminalized ones).

According to the US Department of Labor's Bureau of Labor Statistics, the jobs that have the most fatalities are fishing and hunting workers, logging workers, roofers, and construction workers.[4] (I doubt it is including criminalized occupations.) What these jobs have in common—besides the danger—is that they are low paying and so-called low prestige, since you don't need a formal degree and there is a low barrier to entry. As usual, the people with the least power face the most danger.

Workers not born in the US are especially at risk for being injured or killed at work.[5] In *The Undocumented Americans*, Karla Cornejo Villavicencio tells the story of Harrison Allende, who died in 2012 after working construction near a chemical plant.[6] Allende was reluctant to go to the doctor at first because of the expense. After eventually relenting and being diagnosed with cancer, none of the hospitals would treat Allende because of legal status. Sadly, Allende died not long after being turned away. His example shows us how citizenship status can be determinative of survival.

Cornejo Villavicencio also spoke with workers from Central and South America, many of whom became disabled after working in New York City cleaning up debris after September 11, 2001:

> Paloma has a string of illnesses that are common to all of the cleanup workers—sleep apnea, PTSD, depression, anxiety, gastrointestinal issues. She also has breast cancer. She can't work because her bones hurt, and she often gets fevers, chills, and vertigo....
>
> Aging undocumented people have no safety net. Even though half of undocumented people pay into Social Security, none are eligible for benefits. They are unable to purchase health insurance. They probably don't own their own homes. They don't have 401(k)s or retirement plans of any kind.[7]

Undocumented workers who do become disabled don't even have access to the meager disability benefits available to documented workers.

The current system makes it impossible for poor and undocumented people to survive it, and part of that is creating conditions that encourage disablement and death.

Environmental Racism

Environmental racism refers to the disproportionate effects of disabling environmental conditions on people of color. People of color are more likely to live in neighborhoods built on hazardous sites and where there are higher levels of toxic substances that are known to cause adverse health outcomes.

Dr. Harriet A. Washington examines environmental racism in depth in the book *A Terrible Thing to Waste: Environmental Racism and Its Assault on the American Mind*. One of the substances Dr. Washington looks at is lead. Though many children, especially those in Black communities, are exposed to lead, the government has largely ignored this problem. Washington notes that even though almost all of the at least thirty-seven thousand children in Baltimore who were diagnosed with lead poisoning between 1993 and 2015 were Black, now only one in five Black children in Baltimore is tested for lead.[8]

Lead is common in low-income housing, and children are especially susceptible to poisoning from the toxic substance. Lead is known to be an issue in Flint, Michigan (that *still* hasn't been fixed), but it's also a problem throughout the country. According to Dr. Washington, lead poisoning causes cognitive and learning disabilities, slowed growth, anemia, heart disorders, and many other acute and chronic illnesses.[9] And lead isn't the only disabling substance that people in poor neighborhoods are exposed to. Dr. Washington also chronicled stories of environmental mercury and arsenic poisoning, among others.

Even though race is culturally constructed and not biologically identifiable, it's still correlated with many things that are disabling. This is in part because of the link between race and poverty, and both of those and disability, but those links aren't the whole story. Even when other factors are controlled for, race is correlated with disability and death. Dorothy Roberts wrote about this in *Fatal Invention: How Science, Politics, and Big Business Re-create Race in the Twenty-First Century*, whose thesis is that there is no such thing as biological race:

> There is growing evidence that living in a society that devalues your intelligence, character, and beauty, where you encounter discrimination on a daily basis, and in which entire institutions systematically disadvantage the group you belong to, exacts a toll on health that scientists are only beginning to fathom. . . .

So let me be clear: race is not a biological category that naturally produces health disparities because of genetic differences. Race is a political category that has staggering biological consequences because of the impact of social inequality on people's health. Understanding race as a political category does not erase its impact on biology; instead, it redirects attention from genetic explanations to social ones.[10]

Though low-income white people are of course also affected by living near toxins and hazards, people of color are more likely to live in neighborhoods near waste sites. It cannot be stressed enough how racialized disablement is.

Trauma

Post-traumatic stress disorder (PTSD) is a diagnosis based on experiencing disabling symptoms as a result of trauma. Unsurprisingly, the more trauma someone has experienced, the more likely they are to become disabled.[11] Along with PTSD, people who have experienced trauma are more likely to develop all sorts of physical and mental disabilities.

One famous study looked at the relationship between adverse childhood experiences (ACEs) and health issues, disability, and employment, as well as other outcomes later in life.[12] The researchers defined ACEs to include issues like experiencing or being exposed to violence, parental substance abuse, parental incarceration, and other stressors. High ACE scores were found to correspond with a host of outcomes, including health problems and other disabilities.

While the ACEs study is huge and is relied on by many professionals, I do wonder whether there is some conflation of correlation and causation in the way its findings are interpreted. I think it's often read as saying that ACEs cause illness and disability, which I don't necessarily disagree with. But it is likely that there are also various third factors that cause *both*

ACEs and the outcomes that were measured in the study. In other words, things like capitalism-induced poverty, a widening carceral net, and white supremacy create environments where marginalized people are likely to experience both ACEs *and* disablement.

Either way, we need to think about trauma in a holistic way that addresses the systems that are the root causes of these issues. Trauma doesn't exist in a vacuum.

Trauma can—and after a certain point surely will—cause disability. However, we need to be cautious about all of this, because it's easy to use this information in a way that reinforces the medical model and carceral systems. Trauma is a failure of community—and government—not a problem inside an individual.

It's common now for people in the mental health and adjacent fields to talk about trauma, but "trauma-informed" doesn't necessarily mean anything. To be truly trauma informed, we need to be working on the conditions of society and the government to minimize the trauma that happens to people.

Conclusion

Disabled people are disproportionately caught up in the carceral net, which extends from prison to CPS to the doctor's office to the Environmental Protection Agency. People who are marginalized in other ways are more likely to become disabled or more disabled. Though I've only touched on a few of the many ways this happens, disablement as a concept is an important one as we look at the link between incarceration and disability. If you look at disability and carceral systems as the two circles in a Venn diagram, the overlap grows larger the longer someone is involved in these systems.

We need to center disability justice in abolition, and disability organizations need to fight for abolition, which includes acknowledging and understanding the ways that these systems disable people.

Foundational Sources

Roberts, Dorothy. *Fatal Invention: How Science, Politics, and Big Business Re-create Race in the Twenty-First Century*. New York: The New Press, 2011.

Washington, Harriet A. *A Terrible Thing to Waste: Environmental Racism and Its Assault on the American Mind*. New York: Little, Brown Spark, 2019.

Moving Forward

I hope I've made clear that there is not just one way to work toward abolition, there are infinite ways. To go back to the map metaphor (for the last time—I promise!), when you are navigating to a destination there are lots of different routes you can take. While I always have opinions, I don't know what path makes the most sense for you and your community.

We all have limited capacity and resources and can only focus on so much. My goal with this section—and the book as a whole—is to share some of what I've learned with others working toward abolition—just as they have shared with me in the dozens of books and documents that I've referenced here—so that we can collectively be more effective.

This book focuses a lot on problems, but that's because identifying them is the only way we can solve them. In many of the chapters, I've specifically identified potential changes and abolitionist reforms that can be made or fought for, and others are obvious based on the problem. This chapter contains just a few ideas that may or may not work for you, targeted for the (relative) short term.

People critique abolition because they say it doesn't have realistic next steps, but that's just not true. Those of us who have the most visceral understanding of these issues and proposals to move forward are usually the last ones to be listened to. I wanted to use this chapter to identify some immediate opportunities for praxis.

Remember, we are not limited to what currently exists, and we can create the things we need to make the world we want.

There are infinite ways in which we can work toward abolition, and by centering the most affected, communities can decide what works best for them. Changing things changes things.

Principles

Before I talk about concrete policies, I want to talk about principles. It's crucial to develop an abolitionist analysis that we can apply to different situations to know what to do next in novel and ever-changing conditions. These are concepts that can be used to think about how to put more abolition in our disability justice and more disability justice in our abolition. As always, take what works for you.

Run Upstream—Focus on Systems

For radical change like abolition to happen, we need to dig these systems up by the roots. When we encounter problems in our communities, we need to trace back until we find the source. It may not make strategic sense to target the source at that moment, but we need to understand how our actions fit in with the broader struggle.

Abolition is not a personal growth project. It's not about us becoming good and forgiving people and being nice to our friends. That may happen as we understand the way people are victimized by incarceration, but it should not be our focus. Again, as Mariame Kaba says, "Abolition is not about your fucking feelings." Abolition is about concretely freeing people from carceral institutions and the other systems that are killing us.

If you've read everything up until this point, one thing that should be clear is that the carceral state is not an interpersonal problem and abolition and disability justice both require targeting policies and systems. Making changes that only help individuals one by one won't interrupt the gears of criminalization and white supremacy.

This doesn't mean that a particular person shouldn't devote part (or all) of their time and energy on, for example, getting one person out of prison or saving someone's life. There is a place for interpersonal work, but we all need to understand how it fits into broader systems. How we can be most useful will differ based on the power and resources and connections we have.

Know the Difference between Reformist Reforms and Changes That Bring Us Closer to Abolition

I wrote this book because I believe that political education is a crucial part of abolition. Throughout it, I've used a map analogy to explain the importance of understanding the goal we are working toward in order to be able to accurately pursue it. At the risk of stretching the analogy to the point of breaking, knowing how to tell the difference between reformist reforms and abolitionist reforms is the compass to that map.

Critical Resistance, an organization seeking to end the prison-industrial complex, has a great guide to the problems with many popular policing reforms and how they end up strengthening carceral systems.[1] Critical Resistance has four questions it asks to start thinking about whether a proposed reform is carceral or abolitionist. Though this version focuses on "police," it's applicable across systems.

- First, it asks if the reform reduces funding to the police.
- Then it asks if the reform challenges the notion that police increase safety.
- The third question is whether the reform reduces the tools, tactics, and technologies that police have at their disposal.
- Finally, it asks if the reform reduces the scale of policing.

Body cameras, community policing, more training, civilian review and oversight boards, and jailing police officers who have killed and abused civilians are all "reforms" that actually increase the size and scope of the carceral state. They also don't challenge any of the traditional ideas or structure of policing. Conversely, Critical Resistance identified the following as abolitionist changes: suspending the use of paid administrative leave for cops under investigation; withholding pensions from and not rehiring cops involved in the use of excessive force; capping overtime and pay accrual for military exercises; withdrawing participation in police militarization programs; prioritizing spending on community health, education, and affordable housing; and reducing the size of the police force.

As I stress throughout this book, we need to look at policy proposals closely and make sure they are leading us toward rather than away from abolition. It's not the size of the change that determines whether something is abolitionist, but the effects of it. There are lots of books with tons of different ideas about how to work toward a world without prisons, and the Resources section at the end of this book may be a good place to start. Sometimes it may seem like every proposed intervention is problematic, but there are tons of ways that we can work toward abolition, especially if the concerns of the most affected are taken seriously.

Accessibility

Some of the principles of disability justice lead to obvious opportunities for praxis, with accessibility being especially important. Activism, especially abolition-related organizing, needs to be accessible to disabled people. This is both very complicated and also very simple.

The complicated part of accessibility is that there is no one-size-fits-all solution. Abled people often say something is "accessible" when they mean it is wheelchair accessible or it complies with ADA. This doesn't help someone with chemical sensitivities who gets violently ill around perfumes, or a disabled person who relies on public transportation because they can't drive. Accessibility is an *individualized* determination, and there is no such thing as something being "totally accessible."

That doesn't mean that you can't try and that you shouldn't commit to making things accessible for everyone who wants to attend. While there is no ceiling on the amount of different kinds of accessibility measures that could potentially be put in place, there is definitely a floor. There are helpful checklists on the internet for different kinds of events, and I always recommend hiring a disability or accessibility consultant when possible. It's so easy for the most well-intentioned people—including myself—to forget about things like website accessibility or other aspects of accessibility.

But here's the simple part about accessibility: all you need to do is ask people what they need and then provide it. For so many reasons, people get freaked out about disability and think accessibility and accommodations are some kind of secret disability code language that you need to have a lot of knowledge to understand. It's actually pretty easy: ask people what they need and provide it. That's it! If someone can't do stairs, make sure there are no stairs. If someone needs a chair with no arms, find a chair with no arms. The more accessibility becomes the norm, the easier it is.

For example, even though my illnesses made it impossible for me to attend my local Black Lives Matter protests in 2020, I was able to be useful (and increase accessibility) by fundraising and coordinating the ASL interpreters for the events (from bed). The organizers were grateful to have this resource, especially because I tried hard to make sure they didn't have to do any labor around it. (And obviously I was in contact with the organizers before doing this.) I really appreciated feeling connected to my local community, and the organizers appreciated having better accessibility and one less thing to deal with. Now other (better-funded) local organizations have also started to provide ASL interpreters at events, and it's become more of a norm. Requiring masks is also important for accessibility—and almost free, since you only need to provide masks for those who don't have them. Note that when you do have requirements like these, it is important to enforce them. It's so frustrating to get to an event that has assured me it requires masks only to see a bunch of naked faces, and it puts people at risk (of illnesses as well as wasted time and energy).

Between the checklist accessibility guides and building authentic relationships with the disability *community* (not just individuals) so that everyone—disabled and not—knows how to and feels comfortable asking for whatever they need to participate, the abolitionist movement and disability justice movements can help strengthen each other.

Though this may seem incongruous with the last couple of principles, they actually go hand in hand. I said above that accessibility isn't just for disabled people, it's for everyone. If there are no disabled people in the room—metaphorically, if not literally—then our analysis will be lacking. This whole book is essentially about how much has been overlooked so far because of the lack of disability focus in abolition.

The systems that affect disabled people most won't be identified or targeted without disabled people at the (once again sometimes metaphorical) table. They also won't be abolished without understanding the way that disability affects both incarcerated people and the whole carceral state.

Leadership Too

It's not enough for disabled people to participate in these movements. We need to be leaders. Disabled people are more likely to have lived experiences of carceral systems, so we have unique wisdom and strategies for survival that could help make movements so much more effective. But for that to happen, leadership also needs to be accessible to disabled people.

Often what happens is that someone will get a job at a nonprofit or other organization that funds a certain kind of work, which then puts them in a leadership position. For example, in some of the sex-worker-rights organizing I've done, the "leaders" were those employed by a few different nonprofits that fund this work. So often it is the nonprofits that "choose" movement leaders, putting disabled people once again at a disadvantage. This is not how it should be, as I detail in the chapter on the nonprofit industrial complex, but this is how it is. Because of ableism and inaccessibility, disabled people are much less likely to be employed. And if we are, the demands of full-time employment may make it difficult for us to do anything else besides work. I don't mean making the one visibly disabled person pose in every picture; I mean understanding that there are massive barriers to disabled people being able to have real leadership positions and actually funding and putting resources into disabled leadership. Not for our sake, but for yours.

Flexibility

Even if your budget is zero, as is often the case in this work, you can still do a lot toward accessibility. If you've successfully built connections with the disability community, its members may be willing to help (though we should never be obligated to provide our own accommodations or do any other labor that nondisabled don't have to do to attend). However, one of the biggest and best changes toward disability justice that individuals and organizations can make is just being flexible.

Essentially, an accommodation is an exception to a rule, for example, working from home instead of the office. While capitalism and white supremacy want us to have hard-line rules without exceptions, disability justice and abolition both require context and nuance, and we can embody that.

A lot of times, people like to say no for no reason. Not just to disabled people, but especially to disabled people. I encourage everyone to think about what happens if we just say yes to people as much as possible, or at least as much as is reasonable. Let's understand that people have bodies that run late, that "no food or drink" shouldn't apply to someone's water for their meds or food to prevent a blood sugar crash, and so on. Think about the *actual* consequences of saying yes to the exception that someone is asking you to make. If you have the power to make that decision, use it for liberation.

Don't Call the Police

Some abolitionists believe that being an abolitionist means you can never call the police no matter what. Others, including me, believe that you should almost never call the police but that there may theoretically be situations in which I wouldn't stop someone from doing it. As a queer, disabled sex worker (though white, which is what the police will see), I am sensitive to criminalization, and I really don't see myself calling the police. At the same time, I'm not going to tell someone as criminalized as or more criminalized than me that they can't do something they feel they need to do. Either way, we all agree that you should not call the police as a general matter.

So how do we handle issues without calling the police? That can happen in a lot of different ways, more than I could fit into ten books. One big way we handle it is not by doing more, but by doing less. In fact, by doing nothing. So frequently people—especially white people—call the police due to either conscious or unconscious racism and ableism when there is literally nothing wrong except for a Black person and/or disabled people existing.

Encouraging people not to call the police is also important. When I talk to people about not calling the police, I like to give them my phone number to use. A lot of times, the police are called because someone feels like they need to do *something*, and calling the police is what they have been taught to do. Instead of centering the person who may be in trouble, we focus on our own comfort and our own desire to "help." Calling the police makes bystanders feel like they "helped" even when the individual did not want the police to be called. We can't make decisions based on our personal feelings, but instead what has the best outcomes however an individual defines it. To give people something they can do in the moment, I tell them to call me if something happens so we can problem-solve together around not calling the police. Ideally, we'd have collectively run options.

Sometimes you need to take risks to be safe. Not calling the police may seem like the bigger risk, but it's actually calling the police that leads to the worst outcomes.

Policies
Free and Universal and Appropriate and Noncoercive Medical Care
This could go anywhere in the book, and I mention it in a number of places, but I am putting it here as well because it is a fundamental concept for abolition and disability justice. That concept is access to health care. Everyone should have health care. Not just any health care, but culturally appropriate health care using the best information and resources that exist. The whole system needs to be changed at every level, but being able to get needed health care could help disabled people survive to do the fighting we need to do.

Health care needs to be free. We can create all the "community resources" in the world, but if the people who need them the most can't access them, they are useless. Abolitionists need to think more about health care and the ways we can participate in and contribute to health-care-related activism (which also provides good opportunities for coalition building). We need to think systemically about increasing access for those who need it the most instead of falling victim to reformist reforms that further entrench the medical-industrial complex.

Pay Attention to Benefits
As I've shown throughout the book, the laws around public benefits have huge effects on disabled people. Abolition and disability justice activists need to pay close attention to these regulations and use abolitionist principles to find potential campaign ideas. For example, there has been a recent push to increase the Supplemental Security Income asset limits. This allows disabled people who wouldn't otherwise qualify for SSI to get benefits and gives some disabled people the opportunity

to have a slightly less tiny financial cushion than they could otherwise have. There are lots of ways that public benefits can be made less carceral without expanding the current system. The first step is to pay attention.

Center Anti-Blackness and Colonization

Since Black and Indigenous disabled people are incarcerated at rates significantly higher than other populations, we need to make sure we *always* include race in our analysis of anything involving disability. Ableism and white supremacy are so intertwined that it is impossible (and unnecessary) to tease them apart. If you want to fight white supremacy, you have to engage with the policies that perpetuate it.

Conclusion

It's true that carceral systems are everywhere, and disabled people feel the brunt of their consequences, especially Black and Indigenous disabled people. However, this also gives us a lot of opportunities to both build and tear down to create a society that truly cares for one another, instead of using "care" just as a rationale for incarceration. When we are thinking about how to work toward liberation, we can use both abolition and disability justice as guideposts to identify the way forward.

Glossary

Nothing has made me more hopeful than the increasing interest in prison abolition and disability justice. The last few years have seen a proliferation of books, articles, and social media posts on both of these topics. However, with popularization comes the misuse and dilution of concepts. Take, for example, when people say abolishing the police doesn't mean abolishing the police. Abolishing the police is literally what the concept is called. Of course it means abolishing the police. That said, I want to stress that these are my definitions for the context of this book. Other people may define these words differently. My attempt here isn't to provide official definitions but to make my meaning clear.

Below is a list of some of the words and concepts that I have used in this book. I have tried really hard to break down seemingly complex topics in ways that make them easy to understand. This glossary is just meant to give a quick overview, and I provide important context for these words and concepts throughout the book.

abolitionist reforms—Changes that decrease the carceral state and move us closer to abolition, as opposed to reformist reforms (see below).

both/and—A shorthand that I use to refer to a maximalist orientation toward abolition. This paradigm recognizes that abolition is not about one solution, it's about millions. It also recognizes that several things can be true at the same time, and abolition is not just about tearing down, it is also about creating.

carceral epidemiology—The way the state uses infectious disease as a weapon against people incarcerated in prisons, jails, nursing homes, institutions, and other places where people cannot come and go as they please.

carceral feminism—An ideology that responds to gendered interpersonal violence by increasing the carceral state.

colonization—The process of foreign powers establishing control over Indigenous land and people.

crime—Something that a bunch of rich and usually white and male politicians decided we should put people in prison for (unless one of them does it). There is not necessarily a relationship between crime and harm, and the definition of what is a crime changes all the time.

decriminalization—The repeal of a criminal law that prohibits something.

deinstitutionalization—The movement and process that occurred in the US during the second half of the twentieth century, in which large-scale institutions for people with (certain kinds of) disabilities closed.

disability—A term that continues to change and has different meanings in different contexts and when used by different people, but I generally use it to mean any kind of "difference" that an individual or society considers to be an impairment.

disability justice—A movement and paradigm that emerged out of the work of Sins Invalid. The ten principles of disability justice, as articulated by Patty Berne, are: intersectionality, leadership of those most impacted, anticapitalism, cross-movement organizing, wholeness, sustainability, cross-disability solidarity, interdependence, collective access, and collective liberation.

disability rights/disability rights model—The goal of disability rights is to get disabled people the same legal status and protections that nondisabled people have. Disability rights doesn't seek to disturb the greater power structures and systems.

disablement—The intentional disabling of marginalized people through state action (or inaction).

eugenics—The policy of controlling reproduction in order to create more "desirable" citizens.

healthism—The privileging of health and healthy people and the assumption that everyone can attain and is striving for "health" (which is an incredibly loaded concept). Healthism sees sickness as a moral failing.

institution—A general term for one of a wide variety of residential settings where disabled people are housed in large groups and subject to supervision and control by employees.

institutional bias—When insurance companies, like Medicaid, will only cover medical care in institutions even though the insured could get their needs met through home and/or community care. This forces disabled people into institutions.

marginalization—The process of taking power away from oppressed groups.

medicalization—Turning conditions and behaviors into medical issues that should be labeled and treated.

medical model (of disability)—The medical model sees disability as an individual defect or aberration that should be fixed if at all possible.

neoliberalism—The literal definition of neoliberalism is an ideology that argues for allowing private companies to take over government functions. I use it a little more broadly to mean taking something that should be looked at systemically and changing it into an individual problem to be solved.

peer services—Assistance provided in a context without an inherent power imbalance. Peer services understands that we all both give help and need help sometimes.

reform—A change of any kind.

reformist reforms—Changes that purport to reduce the carceral state but actually grow or strengthen it.

social model (of disability)—The concept that there is nothing wrong with disability, and if there is a problem it is because of the mismatch between the person and environment and therefore the environment should change.

"the state"—Similar to "the government," but broader because it includes those that the government has relationships with.

surveillance—Observation by the state or its collaborators.

transincarceration—Moving from one site of incarceration to another, for example, from an institution to a prison.

Notes

Preface

1   Elisabeth Gawthrop, "The Color of Coronavirus: COVID-19 Deaths by Race and Ethnicity in the U.S.," APM Research Lab, October 19, 2023, https://www.apmresearchlab.org/covid/deaths-by-race.

2   Latoya Hill and Samantha Artiga, "COVID-19 Cases and Deaths by Race/Ethnicity: Current Data and Changes over Time," Kaiser Family Foundation, August, 22, 2022, https://www.kff.org/coronavirus-covid-19/issue-brief/covid-19-cases-and-deaths-by-race-ethnicity-current-data-and-changes-over-time; Matthew L. Bosworth, Daniel Ayoubkhani, Vahé Nafilyan, Josephine Foubert, Myer Glickman, and Calum Davey, "Deaths Involving COVID-19 by Self-Reported Disability Status during the First Two Waves of the COVID-19 Pandemic in England: A Retrospective, Population-Based Cohort Study," *Lancet* 6, no. 11 (November 2021): E817–25, https://doi.org/10.1016/S2468-2667(21)00206-1.

3   "The Catastrophic Cost of Uninsurance: COVID-19 Cases and Deaths Closely Tied to America's Health Coverage Gaps," Families USA, March 2021, https://familiesusa.org/wp-content/uploads/2021/03/2021-37_Loss-of-Lives_Report_AnalysisStyleB_Final.pdf.

4   Katherine Keisler-Starkey and Lisa N. Bunch, "Health Insurance Coverage in the United States: 2021," US Census Bureau, September 2022, https://www.census.gov/content/dam/Census/library/publications/2022/demo/p60-278.pdf.

5   Cara Page and Eesha Pandit, "Intersection of Justice in the Time of Corona Virus," Crunk Feminist Collective, March 31, 2020, https://www.crunkfeministcollective.com/2020/03/31/intersections-of-justice-in-the-time-of-corona-virus.

6   "The COVID Prison Project Tracks Data and Policy across the Country to Monitor COVID-19 in Prisons," COVID Prison Project, accessed November 10, 2023, https://covidprisonproject.com.

7   Rachel Strodel, Lauren Dayton, Henri M. Garrison-Desany, Gabriel Eber, Chris Beyrer, Joyell Arscott, et al., "COVID-19 Vaccine

Prioritization of Incarcerated People Relative to Other Vulnerable Groups: An Analysis of State Plans," *PLoS ONE* 16, no. 6 (2021), https://doi.org/10.1371/journal.pone.0253208.

8   "COVID Data Tracker," Centers for Disease Control and Prevention, accessed November 10, 2023, https://covid.cdc.gov/covid-data-tracker/#trends_weeklydeaths_select_00; Kate Sullivan, Jamie Gumbrecht, Allie Malloy, and Kevin Liptak, "Biden: The Pandemic Is Over," CNN Politics, September 18, 2022, https://www.cnn.com/2022/09/18/politics/biden-pandemic-60-minutes/index.html.

9   Melody Schreiber, "Apocalypse Soon," *New Republic*, October 4, 2022, https://newrepublic.com/article/167946/biden-pandemic-omicron-bivalent-boosters.

10   Associated Press, "Biden Ends COVID National Emergency after Congress Acts," NPR, April 11, 2023, https://www.npr.org/2023/04/11/1169191865/biden-ends-covid-national-emergencyv; "COVID Data Tracker," CDC, accessed November 10, 2023, https://covid.cdc.gov/covid-data-tracker/#trends_weeklydeaths_select_00.

11   Lena H. Sun and Amy Goldstein, "What the End of the COVID Public Health Emergency Means for You," *Washington Post*, May 4, 2023, https://www.washingtonpost.com/health/2023/05/04/covid-public-health-emergency-end.

Introduction

1   Ejeris Dixon and Leah Lakshmi Piepzna-Samarasinha, "Be Humble: An Interview with Mariame Kaba," in *Beyond Survival: Strategies and Stories from the Transformative Justice Movement*, ed. Ejeris Dixon and Leah Lakshmi Piepzna-Samarasinha (Chico, CA: AK Press, 2020), 290.

Abolition Basics

1   Angela Davis, *Are Prisons Obsolete?* (New York: Seven Stories Press, 2003), 16.

2   J. Reiman, "Rich Get Richer and the Poor Get Prison: Ideology, Crime, and Criminal Justice," US Department of Justice, 1995, https://www.ojp.gov/ncjrs/virtual-library/abstracts/rich-get-richer-and-poor-get-prison-ideology-crime-and-criminal.

3   Charles P. Pierce, "15 Years. More Than 1 Million Dead. No One Held Responsible," *Esquire*, March 21, 2018, https://www.esquire.com/news-politics/politics/a19547603/iraq-15-years-george-bush.

4   Alex S. Vitale, *The End of Policing* (London: Verso, 2018), 31.

5   Vitale, *The End of Policing*, 32.

6   Daniel Cooper and Ryan Lugalia-Hollon, "Concentrating

Punishment: Long-Term Consequences for Disadvantaged Places," in *The Long Term: Resisting Life Sentences, Working toward Freedom*, ed. Alice Kim, Erica R. Meiners, Audrey Petty, Jill Petty, Beth E. Richie, and Sarah Ross (Chicago: Haymarket Books, 2018), 125.

7   Mariame Kaba, Josie Duffy Rice, and Reina Sultan, "Uncaging Humanity: Rethinking Accountability in the Age of Abolition," *Bitch*, December 8, 2020, https://www.bitchmedia.org/article/mariame-kaba-josie-duffy-rice-rethinking-accountability-abolition.

8   Victoria Law, *"Prisons Make Us Safer" and 20 Other Myths about Mass Incarceration* (Boston: Beacon Press, 2021), 17–24.

9   Melvin Washington II, "Beyond Jails: Community-Based Strategies for Public Safety," Vera Institute of Justice, November 2021, https://www.vera.org/beyond-jails-community-based-strategies-for-public-safety.

10   Cooper and Lugalia-Hollon, "Concentrating Punishment," 126.

11   Cooper and Lugalia-Hollon, "Concentrating Punishment," 126.

12   "Policing and Racial Injustice: A Disability Rights Perspective Impacts and Solutions," Disability Rights Ohio, accessed December 2, 2022, https://www.ohchr.org/sites/default/files/Documents/Issues/Racism/RES_43_1/NGOsAndOthers/disability-rights-ohio.pdf.

13   Sam Levin, "Seattle Woman Killed by Police while Children Were Home after Reporting Theft," *Guardian*, June 19, 2017, https://www.theguardian.com/us-news/2017/jun/19/seattle-police-shooting-charleena-lyles-mother.

14   Al Baker, J. David Goodman, and Benjamin Mueller, "Beyond the Chokehold: The Path to Eric Garner's Death," *New York Times*, June 13, 2015, https://www.nytimes.com/2015/06/14/nyregion/eric-garner-police-chokehold-staten-island.html.

15   John Woodrow Cox, Lynh Bui, and DeNeed L. Brown, "Who Was Freddie Gray? How Did He Die? And What Led to the Mistrial in Baltimore?," *Washington Post*, December 16, 2015, https://www.washingtonpost.com/local/who-was-freddie-gray-and-how-did-his-death-lead-to-a-mistrial-in-baltimore/2015/12/16/b08df7ce-a433-11e5-9c4e-be37f66848bb_story.html.

16   Alexi Jones and Wendy Sawyer, "Arrest, Release, Repeat: How Police and Jails are Misused to Respond to Social Problems," Prison Policy Initiative, August 2019, https://www.prisonpolicy.org/reports/repeatarrests.html.

17   Rebecca Vallas, "Disabled behind Bars: The Mass Incarceration of People with Disabilities in America's Jails and Prisons," Center for American Progress, July 18, 2016, https://www.americanprogress.org/article/disabled-behind-bars.

18 Liat Ben-Moshe, *Decarcerating Disability: Deinstitutionalization and Prison Abolition* (Minneapolis: University of Minnesota Press, 2020), 150–51.

19 Jared Trujillo and Simon McCormack, "Solitary Is Torture. Corrections Unions Want to Use It More Often," New York Civil Liberties Union, June 7, 2022, https://www.nyclu.org/en/news/solitary-torture-corrections-unions-want-use-it-more-often.

20 Jeffrey L. Metzner and Jamie Fellner, "Solitary Confinement and Mental Illness in U.S. Prisons: A Challenge for Medical Ethics," *Journal of the American Academy of Psychiatry and the Law* 38, no. 1 (March 2010): 104–8, https://jaapl.org/content/38/1/104.

21 Dylan Rodríguez, "Mass Incarceration as Misnomer," in *The Long Term: Resisting Life Sentences, Working toward Freedom*, ed. Alice Kim, Erica R. Meiners, Audrey Petty, Jill Petty, Beth E. Richie, and Sarah Ross (Chicago: Haymarket Books, 2018), 149.

22 Roxanne Daniel, "Since You Asked: What Data Exists about Native American People in the Criminal Justice System?," Prison Policy Initiative, April 22, 2020, https://www.prisonpolicy.org/blog/2020/04/22/native.

23 John Poupart, John Redhorse, Melanie Peterson-Hickey, and Mary Martin, "Searching for Justice: American Indian Perspectives on Disparities in Minnesota Criminal Justice System," American Indian Policy Center, 2005, 29–30, https://mn.gov/mdhr/assets/2005.05%20American%20Indian%20Perspectives%20on%20Disparities%20in%20the%20Minnesota%20Criminal%20Justice%20System_tcm1061-457042.pdf.

24 See, e.g., Mary Annette Pember, "Death by Civilization," *Atlantic*, March 8, 2019, https://www.theatlantic.com/education/archive/2019/03/traumatic-legacy-indian-boarding-schools/584293.

25 Derecka Purnell, *Becoming Abolitionists: Police, Protests, and the Pursuit of Freedom* (New York: Astra House, 2021), 59. Italics in the original.

26 V. Camille Westmont, "Dark Heritage in the New South: Remembering Convict Leasing in Southern Middle Tennessee through Community Archaeology," *International Journal of Historical Archaeology* 26, no. 1 (2022): 1–21, https://www.ncbi.nlm.nih.gov/pmc/articles/PMC7884100.

27 Jefferson Cowie, "How the Slavery-Like Conditions of Convict Leasing Flourished after the Collapse of Reconstruction," Literary Hub, November 22, 2022, https://lithub.com/how-the-slavery-like-conditions-of-convict-leasing-flourished-after-the-collapse-of-reconstruction.

28 William C. Anderson, *The Nation on No Map: Black Anarchism and Abolition* (Chico, CA: AK Press, 2021), 26.

29 Dara Purvis and Melissa Blanco, "Police Sexual Violence: Police Brutality, #MeToo, and Masculinities," *California Law Review* 108, no. 5, https://californialawreview.org/print/police-sexual-violence.

30 Purvis and Blanco, "Police Sexual Violence."

31 Andrea J. Ritchie, *Invisible No More: Police Violence against Black Women and Women of Color* (Boston: Beacon Press, 2017).

32 Melissa Ditmore and Catherine Poulcallec-Gordon, "Human Rights Violations: The Acceptance of Violence against Sex Workers in New York," *Research for Sex Work*, December 2003, https://sexworkersproject.org/downloads/DitmorePoulcallec200312.pdf.

33 Victoria Law, "Against Carceral Feminism," *Jacobin*, October 24, 2014, https://truthout.org/articles/against-carceral-feminism.

34 Law, "Against Carceral Feminism."

35 Beth Richie, *Arrested Justice: Black Women, Violence, and America's Prison Nation* (New York: New York University Press, 2012).

36 Law, "Against Carceral Feminism."

37 Rachel Caïdor, Shira Hassan, Deana Lewis, and Beth E. Richie, "Do We Want Justice, or Do We Want Punishment? A Conversation about Carceral Feminism between Rachel Caïdor, Shira Hassan, Deana Lewis, and Beth E. Richie," in *The Long Term: Resisting Life Sentences Working towards Freedom*, ed. Alice Kim, Erica R. Meiners, Audrey Petty, Jill Petty, Beth E. Richie, and Sarah Ross (Chicago: Haymarket Books, 2018), 166.

38 Val Kiebala, "'It's an Emergency': Tens of Thousands of Incarcerated People Are Sexually Assaulted Each Year," *Appeal*, April 18, 2022, https://theappeal.org/cynthia-alvarado-sexual-assault-in-prisons.

39 "Ending Child Sexual Abuse: A Transformative Justice Handbook," GenerationFIVE, 2017, http://www.generationfive.org/wp-content/uploads/2017/06/Transformative-Justice-Handbook.pdf.

40 Mariame Kaba, *We Do This 'til We Free Us: Abolitionist Organizing and Transforming Justice* (Chicago: Haymarket Books, 2021), 152.

Disability Justice Concepts

1 Jonathan M. Metzl, *The Protest Psychosis: How Schizophrenia Became a Black Disease* (Boston: Beacon Press, 2009).

2 Liat Ben-Moshe, *Decarcerating Disability: Deinstitutionalization and Prison Abolition* (Minneapolis: University of Minnesota Press, 2020), 29.

3 Alison Kafer, *Feminist Queer Crip* (Bloomington: Indiana University Press, 2013), 7.

4 Bureau of Labor Statistics, "Persons with a Disability: Labor Force

Characteristics—2022," news release no. USDL-23-0351, February 23, 2023, https://www.bls.gov/news.release/pdf/disabl.pdf.

5   Sins Invalid, *Skin, Tooth, and Bone: The Basis of Movement Is Our People; A Disability Justice Primer*, 2nd ed. (Berkeley, CA: Sins Invalid, 2019), 15.

6   Ellen Samuels, "Six Ways of Looking at Crip Time," *Disability Studies Quarterly* 37, no. 3 (2017), https://doi.org/10.18061/dsq.v37i3. Italics in the original.

7   Samuels, "Six Ways of Looking at Crip Time."

8   Devyn Springer, "The Anti-Black Pinnings of Ableism," July 23, 2020, interview with Dustin Gibson, *Groundings*, podcast transcript, https://groundings.simplecast.com/episodes/ableism/transcript.

9   Moya Bailey and Izetta Autumn Mobley, "Work in the Intersections: A Black Feminist Disability Framework," *Gender and Society* 33, no. 1 (February 2019), https://doi.org/10.1177/0891243218801523.

History and Principles of Disability Justice

1   Sins Invalid, *Skin, Tooth, and Bone: The Basis of Movement is Our People; A Disability Justice Primer*, 2nd ed. (Berkeley, CA: Sins Invalid, 2019), 16.

2   Shayda Kafai, *Crip Kinship*: *The Disability Justice & Art Activism of Sins Invalid* (Vancouver: Arsenal Pulp Press, 2021), 33.

3   Kafai, *Crip Kinship*, 23.

4   *The Combahee River Collective Statement*, United States, 2015, web archive, retrieved from the Library of Congress on November 10, 2023, www.loc.gov/item/lcwaN0028151.

5   "Kimberlé Crenshaw on Intersectionality, More than Two Decades Later," Columbia Law School, interview, June 8, 2017, https://www.law.columbia.edu/news/archive/kimberle-crenshaw-intersectionality-more-two-decades-later.

6   Moya Bailey, "Misogynoir in Medical Media: On Caster Semenya and R. Kelly," *Catalyst: Feminism, Theory, Technoscience* 2, no. 2 (2016): 1–31, https://doi.org/10.28968/cftt.v2i2.28800.

7   Talila A. Lewis, "Honoring Arnaldo Rios-Soto & Charles Kinsey: Achieving Liberation through Disability Solidarity," *Tu[r]ning into Self*, blog of Talila A. Lewis, July 22, 2016, https://www.talilalewis.com/blog/achieving-liberation-through-disability-solidarity.

8   "Access Denied: Origins of the Hyde Amendment and Other Restrictions on Public Funding for Abortion," ACLU, accessed December 4, 2022, https://www.aclu.org/other/access-denied-origins-hyde-amendment-and-other-restrictions-public-funding-abortion.

9   Leah Lakshmi Piepzna-Samarasinha, "Cripping TJ," in *Beyond*

Survival: Strategies and Stories from the Transformative Justice Movement, ed. Ejeris Dixon and Leah Lakshmi Piepzna-Samarasinha (Chico, CA: AK Press, 2020), 239.

10   Mia Mingus, "Changing the Framework: Disability Justice; How Our Communities Can Move beyond Access to Wholeness," *Leaving Evidence* (blog), February 12, 2011, https://leavingevidence. wordpress.com/2011/02/12/changing-the-framework-disability-justice.

11   Sins Invalid, *Skin, Tooth, and Bone*, 47–48.

12   Sins Invalid, *Skin, Tooth, and Bone*, 25.

13   Mia Mingus, "Changing the Framework."

14   Liat Ben-Moshe, *Decarcerating Disability: Deinstitutionalization and Prison Abolition* (Minneapolis: University of Minnesota Press, 2020), 23.

Sex Work, Disability, and Criminalization

1   "Carol Leigh Coins the Term 'Sex Work,'" NSWP, Global Network of Sex Work Projects, accessed December 4, 2022, https://nswp.org/timeline/carol-leigh-coins-the-term-sex-work.

2   Juno Mac and Molly Smith, *Revolting Prostitutes: The Fight for Sex Workers' Rights* (London: Verso, 2018), 101–2.

3   Melissa Gira Grant, *Playing the Whore: The Work of Sex Work* (London: Verso, 2014), 4

4   Gira Grant, *Playing the Whore*, 5.

5   US Attorney's Office, District of New Jersey, "New Jersey Man Charged with Coercing and Enticing Commercial Sex Workers," news release no. 20-072, February 18, 2020, https://www.justice.gov/usao-nj/pr/new-jersey-man-charged-coercing-and-enticing-commercial-sex-workers.

6   "State Court Snapshot: New York State's Human Trafficking Court," Center for Court Innovation, accessed November 10, 2023, https://cjinvolvedwomen.org/wp-content/uploads/2016/12/HTIC-1pager.pdf.

7   Dean Spade, "Dean Spade: Trickle-Up Social Justice," YouTube, February 15, 2014, video, 4:51, https://amara.org/videos/r45E4s5FcOEl/en/105520.

Short-Term Care

1   Mohit Varshney, Ananya Mahapatra, Vijay Krishnan, Rishab Gupta, and Koushik Sinha Deb, "Violence and Mental Illness: What Is the True Story," *Journal of Epidemiology and Community Health* 70, no. 3 (2016), http://dx.doi.org/10.1136/jech-2015-205546.

2   Cameron Morgan, "The Unacknowledged Crisis of Violence against

Disabled People," Center for Disability Rights, accessed November 10, 2023, https://cdrnys.org/blog/advocacy/the-unacknowledged-crisis-of-violence-against-disabled-people.

3   Irit Shimrat, *Call Me Crazy: Stories from the Mad Movement* (Vancouver: Press Gang Books, 1997), 136.

4   Ji Seon Song, "Policing the Emergency Room," *Harvard Law Review* 134, no. 8 (June 2021): 2649–50, https://harvardlawreview.org/2021/06/policing-the-emergency-room.

5   "Understanding EMTALA," American College of Emergency Physicians website, accessed November 10, 2023, https://www.acep.org/life-as-a-physician/ethics--legal/emtala/emtala-fact-sheet.

6   Song, "Policing the Emergency Room," 2676.

7   Leah Wang, "Rise in Jail Deaths Is Especially Troubling as Jail Populations Become More Rural and Female," Prison Policy Initiative, June 23, 2021, https://www.prisonpolicy.org/blog/2021/06/23/jail_mortality.

8   Alisa Roth, *Insane: America's Criminal Treatment of Mental Illness* (New York: Basic Books, 2018), 157.

9   "988 Suicide and Crisis Lifeline," Federal Communications Commission, fact sheet, accessed November 10, 2023, https://www.fcc.gov/sites/default/files/988-fact-sheet.pdf.

10 Rob Wipond, "Suicide Hotlines Bill Themselves as Confidential—Even as Some Trace Your Call," *Mad in America*, November 29, 2020, https://www.madinamerica.com/2020/11/suicide-hotlines-trace-your-call.

11 Wipond, "Suicide Hotlines."

12 "Suicide and Self-Harm Risk in Criminal Populations," Biomed Central, introduction to special issue, accessed November 10, 2023, https://www.biomedcentral.com/collections/sash.

13 "Long-Term Involuntary Commitment Laws," Policy Surveillance Program, updated May 1, 2016, https://lawatlas.org/datasets/long-term-involuntary-commitment-laws.

14 "Crisis and 5150 Process," Family Education and Resource Center, FAQ page, accessed November 10, 2023, https://ferc.org/crisis.

15 Disability Rights California, "Understanding the Lanterman-Petris-Short (LPS) Act," publication no. 5608.01, accessed November 11, 2023, https://www.disabilityrightsca.org/system/files/file-attachments/560801Ch1.pdf.

16 Jeffrey Goines, "From Burning Man to Bellevue: A Hero's Journey," in *We've Been Too Patient: Voices from Radical Mental Health*, ed. L.D. Green and Kelechi Ubozoh (Berkeley, CA: North Atlantic Books, 2019), 89.

17 Robert Whitaker and Michael Simonson, "Twenty Years after

Kendra's Law: The Case against AOT," *Mad in America,* July 14, 2019, https://www.madinamerica.com/2019/07/twenty-years-kendras-law-case-aot.

18 Judi Chamberlin, *On Our Own: Patient-Controlled Alternatives to the Mental Health System* (Lawrence, MA: National Empowerment Center, 1977), 8.

19 Chamberlin, *On Our Own,* 171.

20 Kelechi Ubozoh, "How My Friends Showed Up: Mutual Aid," in *We've Been Too Patient: Voices from Radical Mental Health,* ed. L.D. Green and Kelechi Ubozoh (Berkeley, CA: North Atlantic Books, 2019), 50.

Long-Term Care

1 Laura M. Maruschak, Jennifer Bronson, and Mariel Alper, "Disabilities Reported by Prisoners: Survey of Prison Inmates, 2016," Bureau of Justice Statistics, Department of Justice, March 2021, https://bjs.ojp.gov/library/publications/disabilities-reported-prisoners-survey-prison-inmates-2016.

2 Laurin Bixby, Stacey Bevan, and Courtney Boen, "The Links Between Disability, Incarceration, and Social Exclusion," *Health Affairs* 41, no. 10 (October 2022), https://www.healthaffairs.org/doi/10.1377/hlthaff.2022.00495.

3 John E. Hansan, "Poor Relief in Early America," VCU Libraries Social Welfare History Project, accessed November 10, 2023, https://socialwelfare.library.vcu.edu/programs/poor-relief-early-amer.

4 Hansan, "Poor Relief."

5 "Parallels in Time: A History of Developmental Disabilities," Minnesota Department of Administration, Governor's Council on Developmental Disabilities, accessed November 10, 2023, https://mn.gov/mnddc/parallels/four/4a/2.html.

6 Manon S. Parry, "Dorothea Dix (1802–1887)," *American Journal of Public Health* 96, no. 4 (April 2006): 624–25, https://doi.org/10.2105/AJPH.2005.079152.

7 Vanessa Jackson, "An Early History—African American Mental Health," excerpted from Vanessa Jackson, "In Our Own Voices: African American Stories of Oppression, Survival and Recovery in the Mental Health System," accessed November 10, 2023, available on Internet Archive at https://web.archive.org/web/20230526165619/https://academic.udayton.edu/health/01status/mental01.htm.

8 Liat Ben-Moshe, *Decarcerating Disability: Deinstitutionalization and Prison Abolition* (Minneapolis: University of Minnesota Press, 2020), 146–47.

9   Bernard Harcourt, "Reducing Mass Incarceration: Lessons from the Deinstitutionalization of Mental Hospitals in the 1960s," *Ohio State Journal of Criminal Law* 53 (2011), https://scholarship.law.columbia.edu/faculty_scholarship/639.

10   Lydia X.Z. Brown, "Bearing Witness, Demanding Freedom: Judge Rotenberg Center Living Archive," on Lydia X.Z. Brown's Laboring for Disability Justice & Liberation website, accessed November 10, 2023, https://autistichoya.net/judge-rotenberg-%20center.

11   Brown, "Bearing Witness."

12   Maya Schenwar and Victoria Law, *Prison by Any Other Name: The Harmful Consequences of Popular Reforms* (New York: The New Press, 2020), 75.

13   Alisa Roth, *Insane: America's Criminal Treatment of Mental Illness* (New York: Basic Books, 2018).

14   Elizabeth Wagmeister, "Britney Spears Claims Father Took Millions, Tried to Pitch His Own Cooking Show during Conservatorship," *Variety*, January 18, 2022, https://variety.com/2022/music/news/britney-spears-father-conservatorship-show-pitch-1235156922.

15   Julia Jacobs, "Spears Said That She Wanted to Have a Baby, but the Conservatorship Would Not Let Her," *New York Times*, September 13, 2021, https://www.nytimes.com/2021/06/23/arts/music/britney-spears-iud-conservatorship.html.

16   Olmstead v. L.C., 527 U.S. 581 (1999).

17   Ben-Moshe, *Decarcerating Disability*, 197.

18   Jeremy Scahill, "Hope Is a Discipline: Mariame Kaba on Dismantling the Carceral State," interview with Mariame Kaba, March 17, 2021, *Intercepted*, podcast transcript, https://theintercept.com/2021/03/17/intercepted-mariame-kaba-abolitionist-organizing.

19   Ben-Moshe, *Decarcerating Disability*, 194.

The Medical System

1   Samantha Artiga and Robin Rudowitz, "Health Coverage and Care for the Adult Criminal Justice-Involved Population," Kaiser Family Foundation, September 5, 2014, https://www.kff.org/uninsured/issue-brief/health-coverage-and-care-for-the-adult-criminal-justice-involved-population.

2   Jessica T. Simes and Jaquelyn L. Jahn, "The Consequences of Medicaid Expansion under the Affordable Care Act for Police Arrests," *PLoS One* 17, no. 1 (January 12, 2022), https://doi.org/10.1371/journal.pone.0261512.

3   Dorothy Roberts, *Killing the Black Body: Race, Reproduction, and the Meaning of Liberty* (New York: Vintage Books, 1997), 65.

4 Buck v. Bell, 274 U.S. 200 (1927).

5 See, e.g., Adam Cohen, *Imbeciles: The Supreme Court, American Eugenics, and the Sterilization of Carrie Buck* (New York: Penguin Press, 2016).

6 Vaughn v. Ruoff, 253 F.3d 1124 (8th Cir. 2001).

7 Dorothy Roberts, *Fatal Invention: How Science, Politics, and Big Business Re-create Race in the Twenty-First Century* (New York: The New Press, 2011), 37.

8 Jael Silliman, Marlene Gerber Fried, Loretta Ross, and Elena R. Gutiérrez, *Undivided Rights: Women of Color Organize for Reproductive Justice* (Chicago: Haymarket Books, 2004), 226–27.

9 Michele Goodwin, *Policing the Womb: Invisible Women and the Criminalization of Motherhood* (Cambridge: Cambridge University Press, 2020), 25–26.

10 Victoria Law, *Who Do You Serve, Who Do You Protect? Police Violence and Resistance* (Chicago: Haymarket Books, 2016), 99.

11 Goodwin, *Policing the Womb*, 132.

12 Goodwin, *Policing the Womb*, 81–82.

13 Robyn Powell, "Carrie Ann Lucas, Disability Rights Activist and Attorney, Dies Following Denial from Insurance Company," Rewire News Group, February 25, 2019, https://rewirenewsgroup.com/2019/02/25/carrie-ann-lucas-disability-rights-activist-and-attorney-dies-following-denial-from-insurance-company.

14 Samantha Artiga, Latoya Hill, Kendal Orgera, and Anthony Damico, "Health Coverage by Race and Ethnicity, 2010–2019," Kaiser Family Foundation, July 16, 2021, https://www.kff.org/racial-equity-and-health-policy/issue-brief/health-coverage-by-race-and-ethnicity.

15 "The Institutional Bias: What It Is, Why It Is Bad, and the Laws, Programs, and Policies Which Would Change It," Autistic Self Advocacy Network, accessed November 10, 2023, https://autisticadvocacy.org/actioncenter/issues/community/bias.

16 Disability Integration Act of 2019, S. 117, 116th Cong. (2019–20), https://www.congress.gov/bill/116th-congress/senate-bill/117/actions.

Drugs

1 "Criminal Justice DrugFacts," National Institute on Drug Abuse, June 2020, https://nida.nih.gov/publications/drugfacts/criminal-justice.

2 Michele Goodwin, *Policing the Womb: Invisible Women and the Criminalization of Motherhood* (Cambridge: Cambridge University Press, 2020), 118–19.

3 "Drug Arrests Stayed High Even as Imprisonment Fell from 2009

to 2019," PEW Charitable Trust issue brief, February 15, 2022, https://www.pewtrusts.org/en/research-and-analysis/issue-briefs/2022/02/drug-arrests-stayed-high-even-as-imprisonment-fell-from-2009-to-2019.

4   Kelly M. Hoffman, Sophie Trawalter, Jordan R. Axt, and M. Normal Oliver, "Racial Bias in Pain Assessment and Treatment Recommendations, and False Beliefs about Biological Differences between Blacks and Whites," *Proceedings of the National Academy of Sciences of the United States of America* 113, no. 16 (April 19, 2016), https://www.ncbi.nlm.nih.gov/pmc/articles/PMC4843483.

5   Maire O'Dwyer, Philip McCallion, Mary McCarron, and Martin Henman, "Medication Use and Potentially Inappropriate Prescribing in Older Adults with Intellectual Disabilities: A Neglected Area of Research," *Therapeutic Advances in Drug Safety* 9, no. 9 (September 2018): 535–57, https://doi.org/10.1177/2042098618782785.

6   Maya Schenwar and Victoria Law, *Prison by Any Other Name: The Harmful Consequences of Popular Reforms* (New York: The New Press, 2020), 57.

7   Alisa Roth, *Insane: America's Criminal Treatment of Mental Illness* (New York: Basic Books, 2018), 145.

8   D. Werb, A. Kamarulzaman, M.C. Meacham, C. Rafful, B. Fischer, S.A. Strathdee, and E. Wood, "The Effectiveness of Compulsory Drug Treatment: A Systematic Review," *International Journal of Drug Policy* 28 (February 2016): 1, https://doi.org/10.1016/j.drugpo.2015.12.005.

9   Kerwin Kaye, *Enforcing Freedom: Drug Courts, Therapeutic Communities, and the Intimacies of the State* (New York: Columbia University Press, 2020), 165.

10 Kaye, *Enforcing Freedom*, 132.

11 Syune Hakobyan, Sara Vazirian, Stephen Lee-Cheong, Michael Krausz, William G. Honer, and Christian G. Schutz, "Concurrent Disorder Management Guidelines: Systematic Review," *Journal of Clinical Medicine* 9, no. 8 (August 2020), https://doi.org/10.3390/jcm9082406.

12 Schenwar and Law, *Prison by Any Other Name*, 59.

13 Kaye, *Enforcing Freedom*, 11.

14 Bonnie Burstow, Brenda A. LeFrançois, and Shaindl Diamond, eds., *Psychiatry Disrupted: Theorizing Resistance and Crafting the (R)evolution* (Montreal: McGill–Queen's University Press, 2014), 37.

15 Irit Shimrat, *Call Me Crazy: Stories from the Mad Movement* (Vancouver: Press Gang Books, 1997), 56.

16 Derecka Purnell, *Becoming Abolitionists: Police, Protests, and the Pursuit of Freedom* (New York: Astra House, 2021), 155.

17   Mariame Kaba and Shira Hassan, *Fumbling towards Repair: A Workbook for Community Accountability Facilitators* (Chicago: Project NIA and Just Practice, 2019), 7.

Social Work

1   Stefanie Lyn Kaufman-Mthimkhulu, "We Don't Need Cops to Become Social Workers: We Need Peer Support and Community Response Networks," *Medium*, June 6, 2020, https://medium.com/@stefkaufman/we-dont-need-cops-to-become-social-workers-we-need-peer-support-b8e6c4ffe87a.

2   Robyn Powell, "Justice for Parents with Disabilities and Their Children," *Regulatory Review*, October 26, 2021, https://www.theregreview.org/2021/10/26/powell-justice-for-parents-with-disabilities.

3   "Protecting the Rights of Parents and Prospective Parents with Disabilities: Technical Assistance for State and Local Child Welfare Agencies and Courts under Title II of the Americans with Disabilities Act and Section 504 of the Rehabilitation Act," US Department of Health and Human Services and US Department of Justice, August 2015, https://www.hhs.gov/sites/default/files/disability.pdf.

4   Robyn Powell, "Parents with Disabilities Face an Uphill Battle to Keep Their Children," *Pacific Standard*, January 3, 2018, https://psmag.com/social-justice/parents-with-disabilities-face-an-uphill-battle-to-keep-their-children.

5   "Parenting with a Disability: Know Your Rights Toolkit," Christopher and Dana Reeve Foundation, May 5, 2016, https://www.ncd.gov/sites/default/files/Documents/Final%20508_Parenting%20Toolkit_Standard_0.pdf.

6   Robyn Powell, "Achieving Justice for Disabled Parents and Their Children: An Abolitionist Approach," *Yale Journal of Law and Feminism* 33, no. 2 (2022): 39, https://dx.doi.org/10.2139/ssrn.3916265.

7   Dorothy Roberts, *Torn Apart: How the Child Welfare System Destroys Black Families—and How Abolition Can Build a Safer World* (New York: Basic Books, 2022), 66.

8   Center for Advanced Studies in Child Welfare, "Parental Disability and Termination of Parental Rights in Child Protection," *Minn Link* 12 (Spring 2015), https://cascw.umn.edu/wp-content/uploads/2015/06/Brief-12-ParentalDisabilityTPR_2015.WEB_a.pdf.

9   Adoption and Safe Families Act of 1997, Pub. L. No. 105-89, 105th Cong. (November 19, 1997), https://www.congress.gov/105/plaws/publ89/PLAW-105publ89.pdf.

10   Alison Walsh, "States Help Families Stay Together by Correcting a Consequence of the Adoption and Safe Families Act," Prison

Policy Initiative, May 24, 2016, https://www.prisonpolicy.org/blog/2016/05/24/asfa.

11 Adoption and Safe Families Act of 1997, H.R. 867, 105th Cong. (1997–98).

12 Lenore M. McWey, Alan Acock, and Breanne Porter, "The Impact of Continued Contact with Biological Parents upon the Mental Health of Children in Foster Care," *Child and Youth Services Review* 32, no. 10 (October 1, 2010): 1338–45, https://doi.org/10.1016/j.childyouth.2010.05.003.

13 Gary B. Melton, "Mandated Reporting: A Policy without Reason," *Child Abuse and Neglect* 29 (2005): 9–18, https://mandatenow.org.uk/wp-content/uploads/2015/11/Melton-2005.pdf.

14 Roberts, *Torn Apart*, 167.

15 G. Inguanta and Catherine Sciolla, "Time Doesn't Heal All Wounds: A Call to End Mandated Reporting Laws," *Columbia Social Work Review* 19, no. 1 (2021), https://journals.library.columbia.edu/index.php/cswr/article/view/7403/4230.

16 Aja D. Reynolds, "I Know Why the Caged Bird Doesn't Sing: Creating a Healing Space for Black Girls to Reclaim Their Bodies," in *Lessons in Liberation: An Abolitionist Toolkit for Educators*, ed. Education for Liberation Network & Critical Resistance Editorial Collective (Chico, CA: AK Press, 2021), 286–87.

17 Shayla Stogsdill, "Children with Disabilities in the Foster Care System," *Orphans and Vulnerable Children Student Scholarship* 4 (2019), https://pillars.taylor.edu/ovc-student/4.

18 Roberts, *Torn Apart*, 141–42.

19 Emma Peyton Williams, "Thinking beyond 'Counselors, Not Cops': Imagining and Decarcerating Care in Schools," in *Lessons in Liberation: An Abolitionist Toolkit for Educators*, ed. Education for Liberation Network & Critical Resistance Editorial Collective (Chico, CA: AK Press, 2021), 322.

Benefits and Charity

1 Bernadette Rabuy and Daniel Kopf, "Prisons of Poverty: Uncovering the Pre-incarceration Incomes of the Imprisoned," Prison Policy Initiative, July 9, 2015, https://www.prisonpolicy.org/reports/income.html.

2 Bernadette Rabuy and Daniel Kopf, "Detaining the Poor: How Money Bail Perpetuates an Endless Cycle of Poverty and Jail Time," Prison Policy Initiative, May 10, 2016, https://www.prisonpolicy.org/reports/incomejails.html.

3 Rabuy and Kopf, "Detaining the Poor," 4.

4 "Improving Outcomes for People with Mental Illnesses Involved in

New York City's Criminal Court and Correction System," Council of State Governments Justice Center, December 2012, https://www.nyc.gov/html/doc/downloads/pdf/press/FINAL_NYC_Report_12_22_2012.pdf.

5   Larry Cata Baker, "Medieval Poor Law in Twentieth Century America: Looking Back towards a General Theory of American Poor Relief," *Case Western Reserve Law Review* 44, no. 3 (1994): 898, https://scholarlycommons.law.case.edu/cgi/viewcontent.cgi?referrer=&httpsredir=1&article=2675&context=caselrev.

6   "Compilation of the Social Security Laws," Social Security Administration, accessed November 10, 2023, https://www.ssa.gov/OP_Home/ssact/title16b/1614.htm.

7   "Spotlight on Resources—2022 Edition," Social Security Administration, accessed November 10, 2023, https://www.ssa.gov/ssi/spotlights/spot-resources.htm.

8   Dylan Rodríguez, "The Political Logic of the Non-profit Industrial Complex," in *The Revolution Will Not Be Funded: Beyond the Non-profit Industrial Complex*, ed. Incite! Women of Color against Violence (Cambridge, MA: South End Press, 2007), 21.

9   Rodríguez, "Political Logic," 37. Italics in the original.

10 Christine Ahn, "Democratizing American Philanthropy," in *The Revolution Will Not Be Funded: Beyond the Non-profit Industrial Complex*, ed. Incite! Women of Color against Violence (Cambridge, MA: South End Press, 2007), 63.

11 "Annual Report Fiscal Year 2022," Wounded Warrior Project, accessed November 10, 2023, https://www.woundedwarriorproject.org/media/1njp04nt/wwp23_2952_mkt_areportd_usletter_nomgf_pages.pdf.

12 Dean Spade, *Mutual Aid: Building Solidarity during This Crisis (and the Next)* (London: Verso, 2020), 7.

13 Spade, *Mutual Aid*, 9.

Disablement

1   Michele Goodwin, *Policing the Womb: Invisible Women and the Criminalization of Motherhood* (Cambridge: Cambridge University Press, 2020), 44.

2   Derecka Purnell, *Becoming Abolitionists: Police, Protests, and the Pursuit of Freedom* (New York: Astra House, 2021), 52.

3   Liat Ben-Moshe, *Decarcerating Disability: Deinstitutionalization and Prison Abolition* (Minneapolis: University of Minnesota Press, 2020), 141.

4   Bureau of Labor Statistics, "National Census of Fatal Occupational

Injuries in 2020," news release no. USDL-22-2309, December 16, 2021, https://www.bls.gov/news.release/pdf/cfoi.pdf.

5 Pia M. Orrenius and Madeline Zavodny, "Do Immigrants Work in Riskier Jobs?," *Demography* 46, no. 3 (August 2009): 535–51, https://doi.org/10.1353/dem.0.0064.

6 Karla Cornejo Villavicencio, *The Undocumented Americans* (New York: One World, 2021).

7 Villavicencio, *Undocumented Americans*, 45, 149.

8 Harriet A. Washington, *A Terrible Thing to Waste: Environmental Racism and Its Assault on the American Mind* (New York: Little, Brown Spark, 2019), 98.

9 Washington, *Terrible Thing to Waste*, 63.

10 Dorothy Roberts, *Fatal Invention: How Science, Politics, and Big Business Re-create Race in the Twenty-First Century* (New York: The New Press, 2011), 119, 129.

11 "Ruderman White Paper on the Criminalization of Children with Non-apparent Disabilities," Ruderman Family Foundation, August 2017, https://rudermanfoundation.org/white_papers/criminalization-of-children-with-non-apparent-disabilities.

12 "Fast Facts: Preventing Adverse Childhood Experiences," Centers for Disease Control and Prevention, last reviewed June 29, 2023, https://www.cdc.gov/violenceprevention/aces/fastfact.html.

Moving Forward

1 "Reformist Reforms vs. Abolitionist Steps in Policing," chart, Critical Resistance, May 14, 2020, https://criticalresistance.org/resources/reformist-reforms-vs-abolitionist-steps-in-policing.

Resources

I fucking love books, and I read a ton in general and did specifically for this project. A big reason I like books is because I am so isolated, and I don't necessarily have access to these conversations in other contexts. I love being able to read further about the things I am interested in, so I wanted to provide a big list for people who want to learn more.

Many books about these topics are (needlessly, in my opinion) overly complicated or hard to read, and I chose the books on this list in part because of their readability. However, some of these books are denser and more academic than others, and it's okay if you don't understand all of it; there are lots of books that I abandoned or chose not to include because of that. Also—since we all have different brains—what might seem straightforward to me may not work for you, and vice versa.

All this said, books in general don't work for a lot of people for a myriad of reasons, which I totally understand! While reading books was very important to my education, I don't want to give the impression that books or reading are a moral imperative or the only way to get information. Some of these titles may be available via audiobook and other formats, and some people have started abolition study groups to help each other understand these concepts, how to implement them, and how they may apply specifically (or not) to their particular community.

I cannot stress enough that this is a *partial* list, and there are many reasons that a certain book may not be included—the most likely being it hasn't come across my radar or I couldn't access or (another big one) afford it. There are also many great books that I didn't include just because their scope didn't fit neatly with the way I chose to organize this book.

All of this is my disclaimer to not take lack of inclusion to mean anything, and of course being on the list doesn't mean I necessarily agree with every single thing in a particular book. I have also limited myself to just books, but there are tons of helpful articles out there as well. The endnotes have a much more comprehensive list of all of the sources I used for this book. This section is for those who may want to go deeper into some of the topics I covered broadly.

Finally, the topics are very general and just a tool to make this list easier to navigate, and many of these books don't fit neatly. In fact, the books included here were chosen in part because they speak simultaneously to several topics I cover.

Abolition (In General)

Abolition Collective. *Abolishing Carceral Society*. Brooklyn, NY: Common Notions, 2018.

Anderson, William C. *The Nation on No Map: Black Anarchism and Abolition*. Chico, CA: AK Press, 2021.

Creative Interventions. *Creative Interventions Toolkit: A Practical Guide to Stop Interpersonal Violence*. Chico, CA: AK Press, 2021.

Davis, Angela Y. *The Meaning of Freedom and Other Difficult Dialogues*. San Francisco: City Lights Books, 2012.

Kaba, Mariame. *We Do This 'til We Free Us*: *Abolitionist Organizing and Transforming Justice*. Chicago: Haymarket Books, 2021.

Kaba, Mariame, and Shira Hassan. *Fumbling towards Repair: A Workbook for Community Accountability Facilitators*. Chicago: Project NIA and Just Practice, 2019.

Levine, Judith, and Erica R. Meiners. *The Feminist and the Sex Offender: Confronting Sexual Harm, Ending State Violence*. London: Verso, 2020.

Purnell, Derecka. *Becoming Abolitionists: Police, Protests, and the Pursuit of Freedom*. New York: Astra House, 2021.

Richie, Beth E. *Arrested Justice: Black Women, Violence, and America's Prison Nation*. New York: New York University Press, 2012.

Stanley, Eric A., and Nat Smith, eds. *Captive Genders: Trans Embodiment and the Prison Industrial Complex*. Oakland: AK Press, 2011.

Thuma, Emily L. *All Our Trials: Prisons, Policing, and the Feminist Fight to End Violence*. Urbana: University of Illinois Press, 2019.

Disability Justice and Theory

Clare, Eli. *Brilliant Imperfection: Grappling with Cure*. Durham, NC: Duke University Press, 2017.

———. *Exile and Pride: Disability, Queerness, and Liberation*. Cambridge, MA: South End Press, 1999.

Kafai, Shayda. *Crip Kinship: The Disability Justice and Art Activism of Sins Invalid*. Vancouver: Arsenal Pulp Press, 2021.

Kafer, Alison. *Feminist Queer Crip*. Bloomington: Indiana University Press, 2013.

Piepzna-Samarasinha, Leah Lakshmi. *Care Work: Dreaming Disability Justice*. Vancouver: Arsenal Pulp Press, 2018.

Russell, Marta. *Capitalism and Disability*. Chicago: Haymarket Books, 2019.

Sins Invalid. *Skin, Tooth, and Bone: The Basis of Movement Is Our People; A Disability Justice Primer*. 2nd ed. Berkeley, CA: Sins Invalid, 2019.

Incarceration and Disability

Ben-Moshe, Liat. *Decarcerating Disability: Deinstitutionalization and Prison Abolition*. Minneapolis: University of Minnesota Press, 2020.

Ben-Moshe, Liat, Chris Chapman, and Allison C. Carey, eds. *Disability Incarcerated: Imprisonment and Disability in the United States and Canada*. New York: Palgrave Macmillan, 2014.

Roth, Alisa. *Insane: America's Criminal Treatment of Mental Illness*. New York: Basic Books, 2018.

Mad Movement/Mental Health

Burstow, Bonnie, Brenda A. LeFrançois, and Shaindl Diamond, eds. *Psychiatry Disrupted: Theorizing Resistance and Crafting the (R)evolution*. Montreal: McGill–Queen's University Press, 2014.

Chamberlin, Judi. *On Our Own: Patient-Controlled Alternatives to the Mental Health System*. Lawrence, MA: National Empowerment Center, 1997.

Green, L.D., and Kelechi Ubozoh, eds. *We've Been Too Patient: Voices from Radical Mental Health*. Berkeley, CA: North Atlantic Books, 2019.

Metzl, Jonathan M. *The Protest Psychosis: How Schizophrenia Became a Black Disease*. Boston: Beacon Press, 2009.

Shimrat, Irit. *Call Me Crazy: Stories from the Mad Movement*. Vancouver: Press Gang Books, 1997.

The Medical System

Goodwin, Michele. *Policing the Womb: Invisible Women and the Criminalization of Motherhood*. Cambridge: Cambridge University Press, 2020.

Nelson, Alondra. *Body and Soul: The Black Panther Party and the Fight against Medical Discrimination*. Minneapolis: University of Minnesota Press, 2011.

Roberts, Dorothy. *Fatal Invention: How Science, Politics, and Big Business Re-create Race in the Twenty-First Century*. New York: The New Press, 2011.

Washington, Harriet. *Medical Apartheid: The Dark History of Medical Experimentation on Black Americans from Colonial Times to the Present*. New York: Anchor Books, 2006.

Police

Davis, Angela J. *Policing the Black Man: Arrest, Prosecution, and Imprisonment*. New York: Vintage Books, 2018.

Maynard, Robyn. *Policing Black Lives: State Violence in Canada from Slavery to the Present*. Black Point, NS: Fernwood Publishing, 2017.

Ritchie, Andrea J. *Invisible No More: Police Violence against Black Women and Women of Color*. Boston: Beacon Press, 2017.

Vitale, Alex S. *The End of Policing*. London: Verso, 2018.

Prisons

Conrad, Ryan, ed. *Against Equality: Prisons Will Not Protect You*. Lewiston, ME: Against Equality Publishing Collective, 2012.

The CR10 Publications Collective. *Abolition Now! Ten Years of Strategy and Struggle against the Prison Industrial Complex*. Oakland: AK Press, 2008.

Davis, Angela Y. *Are Prisons Obsolete?* New York: Seven Stories Press, 2003.

Gilmore, Ruth Wilson. *Golden Gulag: Prisons, Surplus, Crisis, and Opposition in Globalizing California*. Berkeley: University of California Press, 2007.

Kim, Alice, Erica R. Meiners, Audrey Petty, Jill Petty, Beth E. Richie, and Sarah Ross, eds. *The Long Term: Resisting Life Sentences, Working toward Freedom*. Chicago: Haymarket Books, 2018.

Law, Victoria. *"Prisons Make Us Safer" and 20 Other Myths about Mass Incarceration*. Boston: Beacon Press, 2021.

Schenwar, Maya, and Victoria Law. *Prison by Any Other Name: The Harmful Consequences of Popular Reforms*. New York: The New Press, 2020.

Social Services/NPIC

Incite! Women of Color against Violence, eds. *The Revolution Will Not Be Funded: Beyond the Non-profit Industrial Complex*. Cambridge, MA: South End Press, 2007.

Roberts, Dorothy. *Shattered Bonds: The Color of Child Welfare*. New York: Basic Books, 2002.

———. *Torn Apart: How the Child Welfare System Destroys Black Families—and How Abolition Can Build a Safer World*. New York: Basic Books, 2022.

Spade, Dean. *Mutual Aid: Building Solidarity during This Crisis (and the Next)*. London: Verso, 2020.

Other Topics

Dixon, E., and Leah Lakshmi Piepzna-Samarasinha, eds. *Beyond Survival: Strategies and Stories from the Transformative Justice Movement*. Chico, CA: AK Press, 2020.

Education for Liberation Network & Critical Resistance Editorial Collective, ed. *Lessons in Liberation: An Abolitionist Toolkit for Educators*. Chico, CA: AK Press, 2021.

Kaye, Kerwin. *Enforcing Freedom: Drug Courts, Therapeutic Communities, and the Intimacies of the State*. New York: Columbia University Press, 2020.

Roberts, Dorothy. *Killing the Black Body: Race, Reproduction, and the Meaning of Liberty*. New York: Vintage Books, 1997.

Taylor, Keeanga-Yamahatta, ed. *How We Get Free: Black Feminism and the Combahee River Collective*. Chicago: Haymarket Books, 2017.

Washington, Harriet A. *A Terrible Thing to Waste: Environmental Racism and Its Assault on the American Mind*. New York: Little, Brown Spark, 2019.

Index

"Passim" (literally "scattered") indicates intermittent discussion of a topic over a cluster of pages.

dual diagnosis. *See* concurrent disorders

electric shock devices, 96
emergency rooms, 74–76, 113–14
employment, 43, 114
environmental racism, 177–79
eugenics, 92, 107–11

face masks. *See* masks (public health)
"feeblemindedness," 108
feminism, carceral. *See* carceral feminism
fetal protection laws, 113
forced medication, 80, 126–28
forced sterilization. *See* sterilization, nonconsensual or coerced
foster care, 148, 149, 155

Gamble, Clarence, 110
Garner, Eric, 13
gatekeeping by social workers, 142, 143
GenerationFIVE, 26
Gibson, Dustin, 47
Gira Grant, Melissa, 61–62
Goines, Jeffrey, 80
Goodwin, Michele, 111, 113, 121–22, 175
Gray, Freddie, 13
group homes, 98–99
guardianships, 99–100
Gutiérrez, Elena R., 110

Harcourt, Bernard, 94–95
health care, 190. *See also* health insurance; medical system
health insurance, 113–18, 124
Holmes, Oliver Wendell, Jr., 108
homelessness, 176

hospitals: emergency rooms. *See* emergency rooms
hotlines, 77
housing, 138, 156; Section 8, 166–68. *See also* homelessness
human trafficking court (HTC), 66–67

immigrant workers, 176–77
incarceration. *See* prison and prisons
Incite! Women of Color against Violence: *Revolution Will Not Be Funded*, 169–71 passim
Indigenous Americans. *See* Native Americans
inspections. *See* searches and inspections
institutionalization, 86–105 passim; deinstitutionalization, 92–93, 99, 104
insurance. *See* health insurance; Social Security Disability Insurance (SSDI)
interdependence, 56
intersectionality, 43, 50–52
involuntary sterilization. *See* sterilization, nonconsensual or coerced

Jackson, Vanessa, 91–92
jails, 76, 163; health care, 106; mandated drug treatment and, 129, 130, 139; "transincarceration," 93
judge-mandated treatment: drug treatment, 128; inpatient mental health treatment, 87
Judge Rotenberg Center (JRC), Canton, Massachusetts, 96

About the Author

Katie Tastrom is a writer, speaker, sex worker, and former lawyer. Her work has appeared all over the internet and in the anthologies *Nourishing Resistance: Stories of Food, Protest, and Mutual Aid* and *Burn It Down: Feminist Manifestos for the Revolution*. She is based in upstate New York.

ABOUT PM PRESS

PM Press is an independent publisher of critically necessary books and other media—by radical thinkers, artists, and activists—for our tumultuous times. Our aim is to deliver bold political ideas and vital stories to all walks of life and arm the dreamers to demand the impossible. Founded in 2007 by a small group of people with decades of publishing, media, and organizing experience, we have sold millions of copies of our books, most often one at a time, face to face. We're old enough to know what we're doing and young enough to know what's at stake. Join us to create a better world.

PM Press
PO Box 23912
Oakland, CA 94623
www.pmpress.org

PM Press in Europe
europe@pmpress.org
www.pmpress.org.uk

FRIENDS OF PM PRESS

These are indisputably momentous times—the financial system is melting down globally and the Empire is stumbling. Now more than ever there is a vital need for radical ideas.

In the many years since its founding—and on a mere shoestring—PM Press has risen to the formidable challenge of publishing and distributing knowledge and entertainment for the struggles ahead. With hundreds of releases to date, we have published an impressive and stimulating array of literature, art, music, politics, and culture. Using every available medium, we've succeeded in connecting those hungry for ideas and information to those putting them into practice.

Friends of PM allows you to directly help impact, amplify, and revitalize the discourse and actions of radical writers, filmmakers, and artists. It provides us with a stable foundation from which we can build upon our early successes and provides a much-needed subsidy for the materials that can't necessarily pay their own way. You can help make that happen—and receive every new title automatically delivered to your door once a month—by joining as a Friend of PM Press. And, we'll throw in a free T-shirt when you sign up.

Here are your options:

- **$30 a month** Get all books and pamphlets plus a 50% discount on all webstore purchases

- **$40 a month** Get all PM Press releases (including CDs and DVDs) plus a 50% discount on all webstore purchases

- **$100 a month** Superstar—Everything plus PM merchandise, free downloads, and a 50% discount on all webstore purchases

For those who can't afford $30 or more a month, we have **Sustainer Rates** at $15, $10 and $5. Sustainers get a free PM Press T-shirt and a 50% discount on all purchases from our website.

Your Visa or Mastercard will be billed once a month, until you tell us to stop. Or until our efforts succeed in bringing the revolution around. Or the financial meltdown of Capital makes plastic redundant. Whichever comes first.

Nourishing Resistance: Stories of Food, Protest, and Mutual Aid

Edited by Wren Awry with a
Foreword by Cindy Barukh Milstein

ISBN: 978-1-62963-992-5
$20.00   192 pages

From the cooks who have fed rebels and
revolutionaries to the collective kitchens
set up after ecological disasters, food has long played a crucial role in
resistance, protest, and mutual aid. *Nourishing Resistance* centers these
everyday acts of culinary solidarity. Twenty-three contributors—cooks,
farmers, writers, organizers, academics, and dreamers—write on queer
potlucks, rebel ancestors, disability justice, Indigenous food sovereignty,
and the fight against toxic diet culture, among many other topics. They
recount bowls of biryani at a Delhi protest, fricasé de conejo on a Puerto
Rican farm, and pay-as-you-want dishes in a collectively run Hong
Kong restaurant. They chronicle the food distribution programs that
emerged in Buenos Aires and New York City in the wake of COVID-19.
They look to the past, revealing how women rice workers composed the
song "Bella Ciao," and the future, speculating on postcapitalist worlds
that include both high-tech collective farms and herbs gathered beside
highways.

Through essays, articles, poems, and stories, *Nourishing Resistance*
argues that food is a central, intrinsic part of global struggles for
autonomy and collective liberation.

*"This collection of essays offers invaluable frameworks and inspirational
models on how to get food out of capitalist markets and into the hands and
stomachs of all. They fiercely demonstrate how the harvesting, growing,
preparing, cooking, sharing, and eating of food has shaped and reshaped our
cultures, created the social conditions for conviviality, and helped to break
the seclusion and alienation that racist capitalist patriarchies organize. A
must read for all who dream of keeping practices of commoning alive."*
—Silvia Federici, author of *Re-enchanting the World: Feminism and the
Politics of the Commons*

*"A thoughtfully assembled, refreshingly global collection of radical voices
who urge us to reimagine the meaning of the phrase 'food is political.'"*
—Mayukh Sen, author of *Taste Makers: Seven Immigrant Women Who
Revolutionized Food in America*

Mutual Aid: An Illuminated Factor of Evolution

Peter Kropotkin
Illustrated by N.O. Bonzo with an
Introduction by David Graeber
& Andrej Grubačić, Foreword by
Ruth Kinna, Postscript by GATS,
and an Afterword by Allan
Antliff

ISBN: 978-1-62963-874-4 (paperback)
      978-1-62963-875-1 (hardcover)
$30.00/$70.00   336 pages

One hundred years after his death, Peter Kropotkin is still one of
the most inspirational figures of the anarchist movement. It is often
forgotten that Kropotkin was also a world-renowned geographer whose
seminal critique of the hypothesis of competition promoted by social
Darwinism helped revolutionize modern evolutionary theory. An admirer
of Darwin, he used his observations of life in Siberia as the basis for his
1902 collection of essays *Mutual Aid: A Factor of Evolution*. Kropotkin
demonstrated that mutually beneficial cooperation and reciprocity—in
both individuals and as a species—plays a far more important role
in the animal kingdom and human societies than does individualized
competitive struggle. Kropotkin carefully crafted his theory making the
science accessible. His account of nature rejected Rousseau's romantic
depictions and ethical socialist ideas that cooperation was motivated
by the notion of "universal love." His understanding of the dynamics of
social evolution shows us the power of cooperation—whether it is bison
defending themselves against a predator or workers unionizing against
their boss. His message is clear: solidarity is strength!

Every page of this new edition of *Mutual Aid* has been beautifully
illustrated by one of anarchism's most celebrated current artists, N.O.
Bonzo. The reader will also enjoy original artwork by GATS and insightful
commentary by David Graeber, Ruth Kinna, Andrej Grubačić, and Allan
Antliff.

"*Taking aim at both social Darwinists and Romantic dreamers, Kropotkin's
classic text makes plain that the promise of liberation arises from our
collective instinct to cooperate. In this new edition, lovingly illuminated
by N.O. Bonzo, we can see the powerful amplifying effect of mutual aid
firsthand.*"
—AK Thompson, author of *Black Bloc, White Riot*

Resistance Behind Bars: The Struggles of Incarcerated Women, 2nd Edition

Victoria Law with an Introduction by Laura Whitehorn

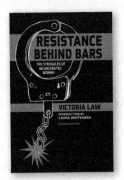

ISBN: 978-1-60486-583-7
$20.00   320 pages

In 1974, women imprisoned at New York's maximum-security prison at Bedford Hills staged what is known as the August Rebellion. Protesting the brutal beating of a fellow prisoner, the women fought off guards, holding seven of them hostage, and took over sections of the prison.

While many have heard of the 1971 Attica prison uprising, the August Rebellion remains relatively unknown even in activist circles. *Resistance Behind Bars* is determined to challenge and change such oversights. As it examines daily struggles against appalling prison conditions and injustices, *Resistance* documents both collective organizing and individual resistance among women incarcerated in the U.S. Emphasizing women's agency in resisting the conditions of their confinement through forming peer education groups, clandestinely arranging ways for children to visit mothers in distant prisons and raising public awareness about their lives, *Resistance* seeks to spark further discussion and research into the lives of incarcerated women and galvanize much-needed outside support for their struggles.

This updated and revised edition of the 2009 PASS Award–winning book includes a new chapter about transgender, transsexual, intersex, and gender-variant people in prison.

"Victoria Law's eight years of research and writing, inspired by her unflinching commitment to listen to and support women prisoners, has resulted in an illuminating effort to document the dynamic resistance of incarcerated women in the United States."
—Roxanne Dunbar-Ortiz

"Written in regular English, rather than academese, this is an impressive work of research and reportage"
—Mumia Abu-Jamal, death row political prisoner and author of *Live from Death Row*

Don't Leave Your Friends Behind: Concrete Ways to Support Families in Social Justice Movements and Communities

Edited by Victoria Law and China Martens

ISBN: 978-1-60486-396-3
$17.95   256 pages

Don't Leave Your Friends Behind is a collection of concrete tips, suggestions, and narratives on ways that non-parents can support parents, children, and caregivers in their communities, social movements, and collective processes. *Don't Leave Your Friends Behind* focuses on issues affecting children and caregivers within the larger framework of social justice, mutual aid, and collective liberation.

How do we create new, nonhierarchical structures of support and mutual aid, and include all ages in the struggle for social justice? There are many books on parenting, but few on being a good community member and a good ally to parents, caregivers, and children as we collectively build a strong all-ages culture of resistance. Any group of parents will tell you how hard their struggles are and how they are left out, but no book focuses on how allies can address issues of caretakers' and children's oppression. Many well-intentioned childless activists don't interact with young people on a regular basis and don't know how. *Don't Leave Your Friends Behind* provides them with the resources and support to get started.

Contributors include: The Bay Area Childcare Collective, Ramsey Beyer, Rozalinda Borcilă, Mariah Boone, Marianne Bullock, Lindsey Campbell, Briana Cavanaugh, CRAP! Collective, a de la maza pérez tamayo, Ingrid DeLeon, Clayton Dewey, David Gilbert, A.S. Givens, Jason Gonzales, Tiny (aka Lisa Gray-Garcia), Jessica Hoffman, Heather Jackson, Rahula Janowski, Sine Hwang Jensen, Agnes Johnson, Simon Knaphus, Victoria Law, London Pro-Feminist Men's Group, Amariah Love, Oluko Lumumba, mama raccoon, Mamas of Color Rising/Young Women United, China Martens, Noemi Martinez, Kathleen McIntyre, Stacey Milbern, Jessica Mills, Tomas Moniz, Coleen Murphy, Maegan 'la Mamita Mala' Ortiz, Traci Picard, Amanda Rich, Fabiola Sandoval, Cynthia Ann Schemmer, Mikaela Shafer, Mustafa Shakur, Kate Shapiro, Jennifer Silverman, Harriet Moon Smith, Mariahadessa Ekere Tallie, Darran White Tilghman, Jessica Trimbath, Max Ventura, and Mari Villaluna.

My Baby Rides the Short Bus: The Unabashedly Human Experience of Raising Kids with Disabilities

Edited by Yantra Bertelli, Jennifer Silverman, and Sarah Talbot

ISBN: 978-1-60486-109-9
$20.00   336 pages

In lives where there is a new diagnosis or drama every day, the stories in this collection provide parents of "special needs" kids with a welcome chuckle, a rock to stand on, and a moment of reality held far enough from the heart to see clearly. Featuring works by "alternative" parents who have attempted to move away from mainstream thought—or remove its influence altogether—this anthology, taken as a whole, carefully considers the implications of parenting while raising children with disabilities.

From professional writers to novice storytellers including Robert Rummel-Hudson, Ayun Halliday, and Kerry Cohen, this assortment of authentic, shared experiences from parents at the fringe of the fringes is a partial antidote to the stories that misrepresent, ridicule, and objectify disabled kids and their parents.

"This is a collection of beautifully written stories, incredibly open and well articulated, complicated and diverse: about human rights and human emotions. About love, and difficulties; informative and supportive. Wise, non-conformist, and absolutely punk rock!"
—China Martens, author of *The Future Generation: The Zine-Book for Subculture Parents, Kids, Friends and Others*

"If only that lady in the grocery store and all of those other so-called parenting experts would read this book! These true-life tales by mothers and fathers raising kids with 'special needs' on the outer fringes of mainstream America are by turns empowering, heartbreaking, inspiring, maddening, and even humorous. Readers will be moved by the bold honesty of these voices, and by the fierce love and determination that rings throughout. This book is a vital addition to the public discourse on disability."
—Suzanne Kamata, editor of *Love You to Pieces: Creative Writers on Raising a Child with Special Needs*

This Is How We Survive: Revolutionary Mothering, War, and Exile in the 21st Century

Mai'a Williams
with a Foreword by Ariel Gore

ISBN: 978-1-62963-556-9
$17.95   224 pages

In *This Is How We Survive: Revolutionary Mothering, War, and Exile in the 21st Century*, Mai'a Williams shares her experiences working in conflict zones and with liberatory resistance communities as a journalist, human rights worker, and midwife in Palestine, Egypt, Chiapas, Berlin, and the U.S., while mothering her young daughter Aza.

She first went to Palestine in 2003 during the Second Intifada to support Palestinians resisting the Israeli occupation. In 2006, she became pregnant in Bethlehem, West Bank. By the time her daughter was three years old, they had already celebrated with Zapatista women in southern Mexico and survived Israeli detention, and during the 2011 Arab Spring they were in the streets of Cairo protesting the Mubarak dictatorship. She watched the Egyptian revolution fall apart and escaped the violence, like many of her Arab comrades, by moving to Europe. Three years later, she and Aza were camping at Standing Rock in protest of the Dakota Access Pipeline and co-creating revolutionary mothering communities once again.

This is a story about mothers who are doing the work of deep social transformation by creating the networks of care that sustain movements and revolutions. By centering mothers in our organizing work, we center those who have the skills and the experience of creating and sustaining life on this planet. *This Is How We Survive* illuminates how mothering is a practice essential to the work of revolution. It explores the heartbreak of revolutionary movements falling apart and revolutionaries scattering across the globe into exile. And most importantly, how mamas create, no matter the conditions, the resilience to continue doing revolutionary work.

"This Is How We Survive *redefines revolution beyond the headline-grabbing events to the everyday resilience of families living under ever-present threats of bombings, assaults, arrests, and disappearances. This book will push you to expand and reimagine your definitions and ideas of revolution.*"
—Victoria Law, author of *Resistance Behind Bars*

The Real Cost of Prisons Comix

Ellen Miller-Mack, Craig Gilmore,
Lois Ahrens, Susan Willmarth, and
Kevin Pyle

ISBN: 978-1-60486-034-4
$14.95   104 pages

**Winner of the 2008 PASS Award (Prevention
for a Safer Society) from the National Council
on Crime and Delinquency**

One out of every hundred adults in the U.S. is in prison. This book
provides a crash course in what drives mass incarceration, the human
and community costs, and how to stop the numbers from going even
higher. This volume collects the three comic books published by the Real
Cost of Prisons Project. The stories and statistical information in each
comic book are thoroughly researched and documented.

Prison Town: Paying the Price tells the story of how the financing and site
locations of prisons affects the people of rural communities in which
prison are built. It also tells the story of how mass incarceration affects
people of urban communities where the majority of incarcerated people
come from. *Prisoners of the War on Drugs* includes the history of the war
on drugs, mandatory minimums, how racism creates harsher sentences
for people of color, stories of how the war on drugs works against
women, three strikes laws, obstacles to coming home after incarceration,
and how mass incarceration destabilizes neighborhoods. *Prisoners of
a Hard Life: Women and Their Children* includes stories about women
trapped by mandatory sentencing and the "costs" of incarceration for
women and their families. Also included are alternatives to the present
system, a glossary, and footnotes.

Over 125,000 copies of the comic books have been printed and more
than 100,000 have been sent to people who are incarcerated, to their
families, and to organizers and activists throughout the country. The
book includes a chapter with descriptions of how the comix have been
put to use in the work of organizers and activists in prison and in the
"free world" by ESL teachers, high school teachers, college professors,
students, and health care providers throughout the country. The demand
for the comix is constant and the ways in which they are being used are
inspiring.

Maroon the Implacable: The Collected Writings of Russell Maroon Shoatz

Russell Maroon Shoatz
Edited by Fred Ho and Quincy Saul
with a Foreword by Chuck D and
Afterword by Matt Meyer and
Nozizwe Madlala-Routledge

ISBN: 978-1-60486-059-7
$20.00   312 pages

Russell Maroon Shoatz is a political prisoner who has been held unjustly for over thirty years, including two decades in solitary confinement. He was active as a leader in the Black Liberation Movement in Philadelphia, both above and underground. His successful escapes from maximum-security prisons earned him the title "Maroon." This is the first published collection of his accumulated written works and also includes new essays written expressly for this volume. Despite the torture and deprivation that has been everyday life for Maroon over the last several decades, he has remained at the cutting edge of history through his writings. His work is innovative and revolutionary on multiple levels:

• His self-critical and fresh retelling of the Black liberation struggle in the U.S. includes many practical and theoretical insights;

• His analysis of the prison system, particularly in relation to capitalism, imperialism, and the drug war, takes us far beyond the recently popular analysis of the Prison Industrial Complex, contained in books such as *The New Jim Crow*;

• His historical research and writings on Maroon communities throughout the Americas, drawing many insights from these societies in the fields of political and military revolutionary strategy, are unprecedented; and finally

• His sharp and profound understanding of the current historical moment, with clear proposals for how to move forward embracing new political concepts and practices (including but not limited to ecosocialism, matriarchy and ecofeminism, food security, prefiguration, and the Occupy Wall Street movement) provide cutting-edge challenges for today's movements for social change.

"This book, Maroon the Implacable, *is that very funky instruction manual on how to make revolution against Imperialist America."*
—Amiri Baraka, former Poet Laureate of New Jersey

Jackson Rising Redux: Lessons on Building the Future in the Present

Edited by Kali Akuno & Matt Meyer with a Foreword by Richard D. Wolff

ISBN: 978-1-62963-928-4 (paperback)
      978-1-62963-864-5 (hardcover)
$24.95/$59.95   584 pages

Mississippi is the poorest state in the US, with the highest percentage of Black people and a history of vicious racial terror. Black resistance at a time of global health, economic, and climate crisis is the backdrop and context for the drama captured in this new and revised collection of essays. Cooperation Jackson, founded in 2014 in Mississippi's capital to develop an economically uplifting democratic "solidarity economy," is anchored by a network of worker-owned, self-managed cooperative enterprises. The organization developed in the context of the historic election of radical mayor Chokwe Lumumba, lifetime human rights attorney. Subsequent to Lumumba's passing less than one year after assuming office, the network developed projects both inside and outside of the formal political arena. In 2020, Cooperation Jackson became the center for national and international coalition efforts, bringing together progressive peoples from diverse trade union, youth, church, and cultural movements. This long-anticipated anthology details the foundations behind those successful campaigns. It unveils new and ongoing strategies and methods being pursued by the movement for grassroots-centered Black community control and self-determination, inspiring partnership and emulation across the globe.

"Jackson is one of the epicenters of resistance for all of us to emulate; this book lays the scene."
—Chris Hedges, journalist, Presbyterian minister, and Princeton University lecturer; author of *War Is a Force That Gives Us Meaning*

"Jackson Rising is the rarest of things: a real strategic plan. You will not find a simple wish list that glosses over the hard questions of resources, or some disembodied manifesto imploring the workers forward, but a work in progress building the capacity of people to exercise power."
—Richard Moser, author of *The World the Sixties Made*

Working It: Sex Workers on the Work of Sex

Edited by Matilda Bickers, peech breshears, and Janis Luna

ISBN: 978-1-62963-991-8
$17.95   240 pages

Fiercely intelligent, fantastically transgressive,
Working It is an intimate portrait of the
lives of sex workers. A polyphonic story of
triumph, survival, and solidarity, this collection
showcases the vastly different experiences and interests of those who
have traded sex, among them a brothel worker in Australia, First Nation
survivors of the Canadian child welfare system, and an Afro Latina
single parent raising a radicalized child. Packed with first-person essays,
interviews, poetry, drawings, mixed media collage, and photographs,
Working It honors the complexity of lived experience. Sometimes
heartbreaking, sometimes hardboiled, these dazzling pieces will go
straight to the heart.

"*If you ever want to know what is really up, talk to a sex worker.* Working
It *is chock-full of harsh realities, hopeful activism, hot takes, sharp writing,
electric intellects, dark humor—all from the culture heroes making their
dollars at the intersection of all our country's worst problems. This is true
outlaw writing, and the stories inside are of crucial importance for us all.*"
—Michelle Tea, author of over a dozen books, including *Rent Girl,
Valencia,* and *Against Memoir*

"*A serious, eclectic collection that takes a critical eye to the tricky questions
surrounding care and work within our society. The thinkers in the pages of*
Working It *have a lot to teach us about both.*"
—Rax King, author of *Tacky,* and co-host of the podcast *Low Culture Boil*

Revolutionary Mothering: Love on the Front Lines

Edited by Alexis Pauline Gumbs,
China Martens, and Mai'a Williams
with a preface by Loretta J. Ross

ISBN: 978-1-62963-110-3
$17.95   272 pages

Inspired by the legacy of radical and queer
black feminists of the 1970s and '80s,
Revolutionary Mothering places marginalized mothers of color at the
center of a world of necessary transformation. The challenges we face as
movements working for racial, economic, reproductive, gender, and food
justice, as well as anti-violence, anti-imperialist, and queer liberation,
are the same challenges that many mothers face every day. Oppressed
mothers create a generous space for life in the face of life-threatening
limits, activate a powerful vision of the future while navigating tangible
concerns in the present, move beyond individual narratives of choice
toward collective solutions, live for more than ourselves, and remain
accountable to a future that we cannot always see. *Revolutionary
Mothering* is a movement-shifting anthology committed to birthing new
worlds, full of faith and hope for what we can raise up together.

Contributors include June Jordan, Malkia A. Cyril, Esteli Juarez, Cynthia
Dewi Oka, Fabiola Sandoval, Sumayyah Talibah, Victoria Law, Tara
Villalba, Lola Mondragón, Christy NaMee Eriksen, Norma Angelica
Marrun, Vivian Chin, Rachel Broadwater, Autumn Brown, Layne Russell,
Noemi Martinez, Katie Kaput, alba onofrio, Gabriela Sandoval, Cheryl
Boyce Taylor, Ariel Gore, Claire Barrera, Lisa Factora-Borchers, Fabielle
Georges, H. Bindy K. Kang, Terri Nilliasca, Irene Lara, Panquetzani,
Mamas of Color Rising, tk karakashian tunchez, Arielle Julia Brown,
Lindsey Campbell, Micaela Cadena, and Karen Su.

"This collection is a treat for anyone that sees class and that needs to learn
more about the experiences of women of color (and who doesn't?!). There
is no dogma here, just fresh ideas and women of color taking on capitalism,
anti-racist, anti-sexist theory-building that is rooted in the most primal
of human connections, the making of two people from the body of one:
mothering."
—Barbara Jensen, author of *Reading Classes: On Culture and Classism in
America*

The Warehouse:
A Visual Primer on Mass Incarceration

James Kilgore and Vic Liu

ISBN: 979-8-88744-042-2
$24.95   208 pages

Mass incarceration is a lived, sensory experience.

The most eye-popping statistics alone cannot relate the enormity of its psychological and societal impacts. This concise, illustrated primer is a collaboration between one of mass incarceration's sharpest opponents, James Kilgore, and information artist Vic Liu. It brings to life the histories and means of daily survival of the marginalized people ensnared in this racist, ableist system of class-based oppression. The book elegantly weaves together the most insightful activist scholarship with vivid testimonials by incarcerated people as they fight back against oppression and imagine freedom.

Those targeted for incarceration do not simply submit to a monochromatic existence behind bars. *The Warehouse* showcases the abolition futures being crafted from the inside as people resist through direct action and artistic expression. This book is designed to inform, enrage, and ultimately inspire the same radical hope propelling incarcerated underminers of the carceral state.

"This book vividly activates the senses in its sharp, accessible, and principled analysis of the scope and scale of the carceral state. From cops to cages, from 'get tough' politics to the economics of phone calls, e-carceration, and rural prison building, and from incremental legislative reforms to the visionary organizing of abolitionists, Kilgore and Liu break down the contours of this warehouse and illuminate our paths toward dismantling it."
—Judah Schept, author of *Coal, Cages, Crisis: The Rise of the Prison Economy in Central Appalachia*

"A visually stunning primer on how the US became the world's incarceration nation. Read it and learn how the criminal punishment system works, whom it affects, and what we, as a society, could be doing instead."
—Victoria Law, author of *"Prisons Make Us Safer" and 20 Other Myths about Mass Incarceration*